... *Equality Illusion* and founder

... UK Feminista. In 2014 *The Equality Illusion* was ... as a key text in the development of the play *Blurred Lines*, written by Nick Payne and directed by Carrie Cracknell, premiering at the National Theatre. In 2010 Kat was named in the *Guardian* as 'the most influential young feminist in the country' and in 2011 she was selected as one of the *Observer*'s 50 contemporary innovators, described as 'Game-changers whose vision is transforming the world around us'.

Further praise for *Pimp State*:

'A full-throated roar against commercial porn and prostitution . . . The simplicity and straightforwardness of its arguments come across as almost restful: demand for the sex-trade is not inevitable; objecting to it does not make you a pearl-clutching prude. Consent cannot be purchased and the porn industry exploits its workers and normalises sexual violence.' Helen Lewis, *New Statesman*

'*Pimp State* is a detailed account of the case against the sex industry, and for the Nordic model: tightly argued, closely evidenced, and persuasive in its call to action . . . Methodically and thoroughly, Banyard dismantles the "myths" that support this presumption. *Pimp State* doesn't limit itself to activities conventionally regarded as prostitution. Instead, Banyard is concerned with the entire field of commercial sexual services, including lap dancing and pornography . . . There are many who would like to establish a pimp state in the UK, but Banyard shows why they must be stopped, and how to stop them.' Sarah Ditum, *G*

'Sex buyers are not the single loners they were often assumed to be in the past. As Kat Banyard demonstrates in her excoriating account of the modern trade in women's bodies, they seek variety, sex acts they can't get in voluntary relationships and, above all, power . . . The debate has become poisonous and Banyard's book provides a much-needed corrective, skewering the myths promoted by the commercial industry with forensic intelligence . . . By putting equality and human rights at the heart of this vital debate, she has done us a tremendous service.' Joan Smith, *Observer*

'The most chilling aspect of 2016's Oscar-winning film *Spotlight*, about the uncovering of large-scale sexual abuse in the Catholic Church in Boston, was how the whole scandal was right under journalists' noses, hiding in plain sight. People knew. *Pimp State*, a barnstorming polemic against the horrors of the sex industry (porn, lap-dancing and prostitution) filled me with a similar sense of unease . . . I challenge anyone to read this book and not feel there is something profoundly immoral and wrong about all of this. And it is there in plain sight.' Eleanor Mills, *Sunday Times*

'Banyard's most useful addition to the debate is attacking the myth that prostitution is just a job . . . What shines through this uncompromising book is an optimism about change. Domestic violence and compulsory "conjugal rights" were once seen as normal, a husband's due. And there are laws against undesirable transactions such as selling human organs or entering into bonded labour contracts. So why not prostitution?' Janice Turner, *The Times*

---

by the same author

THE EQUALITY ILLUSION

PIMP STATE

Sex, Money and
the Future of Equality

KAT BANYARD

FABER & FABER

First published in 2016
by Faber & Faber Limited
Bloomsbury House
74–77 Great Russell Street
London WC1B 3DA
This paperback edition first published in 2017

Typeset by Faber & Faber Limited
Printed in the UK by CPI Group (UK) Ltd, Croydon, CR0 4YY

A CIP record for this book
is available from the British Library

ISBN 978–0–571–27823–7

FSC
www.fsc.org
MIX
Paper from
responsible sources
FSC® C020471

2 4 6 8 10 9 7 5 3 1

With love and thanks to Dorothy Banyard

Contents

Introduction

'Would you mind stepping outside?'

Not wanting to draw more attention to myself, I did as the official whispering in my ear asked. I got up from my seat and tried to look surprised, though unconcerned, as I was escorted out of the conference room.

Out in the corridor the event official turned to me. 'I just want to make sure 'cause we've had some situations. Are you here with a company?'

The woman didn't elaborate on what 'situations' had occurred, but I knew what she was referring to. Three days earlier, delegates arriving here at XBIZ EU, a pornography trade conference held in London, had received a rather unceremonious welcome from a group of feminist protestors. Now the mere presence of one youngish-looking woman on her own was apparently enough to make the organisers twitchy.

But why should a single woman stick out like a sore thumb at a porn industry meet-up? After all, the world's most famous porn peddler, Hugh Hefner, has argued that '*Playboy* and the Playboy clubs were the end of sexism. Women were being held in bondage for hundreds of years, owned first by their fathers and then by their husbands. *Playboy* helped to change all that. That's what the sexual revolution was all about.'[1] As the supposed lucky beneficiaries, shouldn't women and girls

I

have been queuing around the block to find out what new developments in the porn industry would help keep patriarchy at bay?

Hefner portrayed himself as a women's rights pioneer, straight-faced, to a reporter quizzing him in 2011 about protests against his new Playboy Club in London. They had been organised by the pressure group Object and UK Feminista, an organisation I'd set up the previous year, precisely because the engine rooms of the real revolution Hef helped inspire – the global expansion of the sex trade – are not packed out by the grateful daughters of feminism. They are filled with the people I sat among that day in 2013 when I attended the porn trade conference: businessmen. (As it transpired, I was allowed to return to the meeting room after I reassured the organisers I was there for research, rather than placard-waving purposes.)

The conference was hosted at the four-star Radisson Blu Edwardian Bloomsbury Street Hotel. This high-end setting was a testament to how far the porn trade has travelled. Once deemed the preserve of seedy backstreets, the pornography industry has bulldozed its way into the mainstream, and on to Wall Street. In 2011, US investment fund Colbeck Capital Management gave a $362 million loan to a porn company.[2] That company was Manwin (since renamed MindGeek), a sprawling multinational corporation with over thirty-five subsidiaries and which owns some of the most heavily visited porn websites in the world: Brazzers, Pornhub and YouPorn.[3] The man who built this porn empire was Fabian Thylmann, a computer programmer whose online ventures were generat-

2

ing millions of dollars while he was still in his twenties[4] and saw him dubbed 'the Mark Zuckerberg of porn'.[5]

Casting a wistful eye over his long career, eighty-four-year-old Hugh Hefner reminisced in 2010, 'The criticisms that troubled me the most came from the feminists, from liberals, at the very beginning. I was blindsided by them and didn't know what they were talking about.'[6] But the *Playboy* founder was resolute as to who had come out on top. 'I think my critics are dead wrong. It was clear to me then; it's clearer to me today, because I think history has proven me right . . . I've won. We now live in a *Playboy* world.'

Hefner's claim can't easily be written off as mere delusion of grandeur. Pornography has never been more easily, cheaply or heavily consumed as it is today. You can buy *Playboy* magazine from high-street shops, go to a Playboy Club, visit Playboy Online, and watch Playboy TV on cable and satellite. The websites owned by Manwin (now MindGeek) alone are reported to clock up around 16 billion visits each month,[7] while over $1 billion in transactions are processed each year by Ron Cadwell's firm CCBill – the PayPal of porn and go-to online billing company for porn sites.[8] The findings of a recent BBC survey, then, that a quarter of young people have watched pornography by the time they reach their teens, come as little surprise.[9]

Pornography isn't the only part of the sex trade to have experienced a boom over the past two decades. During this time, the number of women paid for sex in Germany's prostitution trade is thought to have doubled, with the current figure pegged at 400,000.[10] The proportion of men in the UK who have paid for sex almost doubled during the 1990s, from one in twenty to nearly one in ten,[11] while UK lap-dancing clubs increased ten-fold between 1997 and 2011.[12] One strip club chain, Spearmint Rhino, today racks up annual sales of nearly $200 million, according to CEO John Gray.[13]

As the sex trade has ballooned, inevitably its influence on popular culture has too. Sometimes that influence isn't just a knowing nod from advertisers, or a borrowed motif in a music video, it's a direct fusion of the two worlds. In 2005, HBO launched *Cathouse: The Series*,[14] which documented daily life at the Moonlite BunnyRanch, a legal brothel in Nevada. Its owner, Dennis Hof, explained the benefits of this exposure to an interviewer: 'Our clients, our friends, can watch our TV show, see us at an award show, and say, "Wow, that Air-force Amy is looking really good. I'm gonna go to the Bunny-Ranch." That's what the success of our show is . . . that finally these are goals that are attainable for the average man . . . I've taken prostitution from guilt and shame to glamour and fame.'[15]

Pointing out that the sex trade generates substantial profits or that it has secured a firm foothold in the cultural mainstream is not a source of great controversy. How societies should respond *is*. Indeed, how the state should deal with this trade is shaping up to be one of the big debates of our time. Should it be legal to pay for sex? What's the best way to promote the safety of women involved? How does online porn impact on boys' attitudes towards women and sex? Is this an industry that is irredeemably sexist or something we should accommodate? In essence, are feminism and the sex trade on a collision course? These are questions that go to the very heart of society's notions of sexual consent, violence and equality.

In recent years a consensus has begun to form around the idea that the sex trade and sex equality can in fact be comfortable bedfellows. Few would deny that the sex trade currently has a sexist side. But then, the argument follows, don't all industries? The proposition that the two are compatible allows room for multiple interpretations: at euphoric best, the sex trade represents the promised land of feminism (see Hugh Hefner's previous 'end of sexism' proclamation). At worst, its present outputs merely reflect misogynistic attitudes in wider society. Somewhere in the middle, the trade is afforded a more mundane profile: that of ordinary work. Yet however sexist it is currently considered to be, what these interpretations share is the underlying presumption that the sex trade is compatible with feminism; that we needn't work to end it; that it can be *reformed*.

The medium is the message

The claim that building a feminist future does not necessitate the abolition of the sex trade is not some esoteric, ivory tower hypothesis. It's a contention that today underpins a global bid for governments to accept, regulate and accommodate the trade. This book is a challenge to that bid. I will show that it is only possible to maintain that the sex trade is compatible with equality between women and men through the creation and retelling of toxic myths: the myth that men paying women to perform sex acts on them is a harmless consumer transaction, on a par with him paying her to serve a cappuccino, dry clean his clothes, or perform any number of other service jobs. The myth that pornography is mere fantasy, not 'real life', and that all we have to do is teach young people how to differentiate between the two. The myth that the sex trade can be made safe, and that the route to get there is by making paying for sex, pimping and brothel-keeping legal. And the myth that any sexism in the sex trade is merely a problem with the message (directors instructing male porn performers to use misogynistic language, say), not the medium itself (sexual consent that was 'purchased', in a brothel or on a porn set).

These myths are being used to create a culture and set of laws that encourage and facilitate men's paid sexual access to women's bodies: what I call a pimp state. It is being pursued most explicitly and literally in the call for governments to take a direct financial cut from the transaction – by licensing brothels, imposing rules on the people inside, and taxing them.

In 2004 MTV aired the first series of *Pimp My Ride*,[16] a show which revolved around a run-down car being done-up and customised: 'pimped'. Appropriately enough, the trade from which that term was borrowed has been given its own makeover, refashioned as a friend to feminism, or at least a benign associate. And for good reason. Because the reality

6

behind these myths is far less convenient for the trade's 'customers' and third-party profiteers, like those attending the XBIZ EU conference. The demand that drives the sex trade is both a cause and a consequence of inequality between women and men, not an inevitable fact of life.

Regardless of the varying ways it is marketed, the sex trade boils down to a very simple product concept: an individual – usually a man – can pay to have a sexual interaction with someone – usually a woman – who doesn't freely want to have it with him. As I'll explore later, there are a bunch of reasons why she may have agreed to it: for Mia de Faoite, whom I met during the course of my research, it was a drug addiction that first lead her on to the streets of Dublin to spend six years being paid by men for sex. For Crystal, who spent over five years as an escort and in brothels, it was a violent boyfriend who first started pimping her. Addiction, pressure from a pimp, an overwhelming sense that there is no other option; there are a multitude of factors that may explain why she's there. But not one of them absolves the actions of the buyer: in the sex trade, the fact that the sexual interaction is not taking place because of mutual desire for emotional or sexual satisfaction is explicit and fundamental to the act – otherwise he wouldn't have to pay her to be there. The sex trade manufactures consent; the result is commercial sexual exploitation on an industrial scale.

So it is understandable why third parties who enjoy the profits and 'consumers' who enjoy the privilege would find common cause in masking this reality with myths. The narrative they peddle has acquired mainstream credibility and little resistance, in part because of a fear and smear campaign that frequently goes hand in hand with it. Those who dare to question the compatibility of the sex trade and sex equality are commonly derided as conservative, anti-sex ideologues. The result is we are spectacularly failing as a society to confront the full reality of sexism at the core of the sex trade. And we will have to confront that reality if we are even remotely serious about wanting equality between women and men. That also means not ducking the fact that in this trade it is overwhelmingly heterosexual men who are the consumers and women who constitute the product. As sex trade scholar Professor Karen Boyle points out, 'the success of the porn industry largely depends upon the willingness of heterosexual men to buy its products, to enter into a contract which provides them with (vicarious) use of a female body for their arousal or amusement.'[17] Same goes for stripping and prostitution, except there the use isn't vicarious. It is an overwhelmingly and inescapably gendered phenomenon. This book reflects that reality.

'If you don't like it, don't buy it' doesn't wash when it comes to the sex trade. Inequality between women and men is needed for patriarchal power plants like Dennis Hof's brothels to operate. It is also an inevitable by-product of that operation. 'We change people's ideas a day at a time . . . one person at a time. We win them over,'[18] Hof has claimed. He is confident of his power to shape attitudes beyond the high white fence surrounding the Moonlite BunnyRanch,[19] which, given the brothel's media exposure, isn't without grounds. As someone whose exploits rely on the state to sanction them, the wider community to tolerate them, and the desire of some men to pay for them, Hof understands better than many that his industry does not operate in a social vacuum. The PR pursuits, daily operations and underlying logic of the sex trade communicate very public, and very powerful, messages.

In turn, society's collective response to the trade is a didactic display in itself. Right now we live in a world in which it is estimated that one in five women will be raped or subjected to an attempted rape during their lifetime.[20] A survey of young people in England found that over four in ten girls aged thirteen to seventeen had been coerced into sex acts.[21] For too many men and boys, the question of whether a woman or girl shares his desire for a sexual interaction is either irrelevant, or that mutuality unwanted. The global sex trade is built on the assertion that it is irrelevant whether the desire to have sex is mutual, as long as he pays, and she feels sufficiently compelled to accept the money. The money isn't coincidence; it's coercion. How we respond to the core message of the sex trade speaks volumes about how seriously society takes violence against all women.

Be in no doubt about the scale of what's at stake. At a period in history when most (though certainly not all) countries are adding laws to the statute books that at least formally assert gender equality, the sex trade is making a concerted bid for states to re-inscribe the sexual subjection of women, albeit somewhat more between the lines this time. Because responding to the present demand for the sex trade by boosting, not blocking, the ability of pimps and pornographers to pump out profits from it re-institutionalises male sexual entitlement – that antediluvian cultural current that says men have a right to access women's bodies, regardless of whether the desire is mutual. It is the collective arms of the state responding to violence against women not by dampening down the conditions for it, but by putting a rocket up it – by helping to attach a profit motive.

In her 1949 landmark work, *The Second Sex*, Simone de Beauvoir wrote, 'what peculiarly signalises the situation of woman is that she – a free and autonomous being like all human creatures – nevertheless finds herself living in a world where men compel her to assume the status of the Other. They propose to stabilise her as an object.'[22] The sexual objectification of women embodied and encouraged by the sex trade has become a central social force serving to 'stabilise her as an object', supercharged by the pursuit of profit. The industry entails the direct sexual abuse of some women, while simultaneously powering a toxic culture of objectification that affects all women. In the story of the status of woman, the sex trade is no side-show.

A pimp state – a society where commercial sexual exploitation is promoted, not prevented – is not one where women and men can live as equals.

It is a state that we can – and must – change.

MYTH 1: Demand for the sex trade is inevitable

But whatsoever is the object of any man's appetite or desire; that is it, which he for his part calleth *good*.

THOMAS HOBBES, 1651[1]

To want to abolish prostitution is like wanting to abolish rain.

NICOLAS BEDOS, actor and director, 2014[2]

It has no beginning and it will have no end. Global demand for the sex trade supposedly flows direct from the very laws of nature. Like it or loathe it, the history of the sex trade is the history of humanity, so the story goes. Natural, necessary, inevitable. And woe betide anyone who tries to get in the way of that demand. In AD 386 St Augustine, a major figure in the early development of Christianity, warned, 'If you do away with harlots, the world will be convulsed with lust.'[3] Though not forecasting fall-out of quite such apocalyptic proportions, the man sometimes dubbed the 'father of modern criminology',[4] Cesare Lombroso, nonetheless concluded in 1893 that the sex trade 'is socially useful as an outlet for male sexuality and a preventative of male crime'.[5]

Fast forward to 2014 and pretty much the same line was trotted out to me over the phone by a sex buyer, who I was interviewing as research for this book: 'As a man I absolutely crave it sometimes. And it's far better that men should avail themselves of these services than go out and commit a crime.'

What crimes did he anticipate? I asked him. 'Well, obviously rape. Even sex crimes against children. So it's far better that they be able to satisfy their urges in this way.' The same year this sex buyer told me of men's helplessness in the face of their sexual desires, a judge in the UK told a man convicted of rape, 'You just lost control of normal restraint . . . She was a pretty girl who you fancied. You simply could not resist.'[6]

If you look back at the everyday lives of men over the past millennia or two, it becomes clearer why this idea gained credibility. It's really not surprising that so many should have believed for so long that men have an uncontainable sex drive requiring release given the frankly appalling number of men who have suffered serious injury and even on occasion spontaneously combusted from not having enough sex. Oh wait, that's right – it's always been fantastical bollocks. So fantastical, in fact, that its power to prop up claims of the sex trade's permanence is now, thankfully, limited. Clearly, this pernicious idea still trips off some people's tongues, and with potentially devastating consequences. Yet the remarks of the aforementioned judge were at least widely condemned in the media;[7] the suggestion that men can't control their sexual urges was recognised for the 'rape myth' that it is, functioning to absolve the rapist of responsibility for his actions.

However, where the notion of the sex trade as necessary outlet for men's uncontrollable desires now falls short, another fairy tale is on hand to help bolster the trade's outward appearance of inevitability. In 2014, *The Economist* magazine ran a front-page story on 'The sex business: how technology is liberating the world's oldest profession.' The final three words of this headline have, of course, become a synonym for prostitution. The subtext was spelt out later on in the feature in the blank assertion that 'the sex trade will always exist'.[8]

The coupling of 'oldest profession' with the sex trade has been traced back to the opening line of Rudyard Kipling's story about a woman involved in prostitution, 'On the City Wall', published in 1889: 'Lalun is a member of the most ancient profession in the world.'[9] However, the mantle of oldest profession was assigned to an assortment of other trades prior to Kipling's use of it. In 1823, for instance, a book published in London featured the following 'ditty in commendation of the Merchant-Tailors' Trade':

> When *Adam* and *Eve* out of *Eden* were hurl'd,
> They were at that time king and queen of the world:
> Yet this royal Couple were forced to play
> The *Taylers*, and put themselves in green Array;
> For Modesty and for Necessity's sake
> They had Figs for the Belly, and Leaves for the Back;
> And afterward Clothing of Sheep-skins they made
> Then judge if a *Tayler* was not the first Trade,
>   The oldest Profession; and they are but Raylers,
>   Who scoff and deride men that be *Merchant-Taylers*.[10]

Today, 'the oldest profession' is a euphemism rarely uttered in total seriousness. If actually subject to any scrutiny it is liable to prompt furrowed brows and questions like, 'Could prostitution qualify as a profession?', 'Didn't hunting and gathering come first?', 'What about tool making? Or farming?' Ultimately, though, the accuracy of the phrase doesn't matter: it does not rely on the precise aetiology of the sex trade for its power to influence. 'The oldest profession' conveys a general sense that the sex trade is beyond our control. Its transhistorical air lifts the assertion above more earthly justifications like beginning dates and biological drives. The sex trade somehow *just is* and always *will be*.

Floating 'up there', it is also untethered from basic logic. When assessing whether something is harmful or not, sexist or not, the question of how long it has been going on is irrelevant. Take murder, for instance; hardly a recent phenomenon among human beings. But that doesn't mean a murderer's actions are deemed more acceptable as a result. It doesn't make us any less inclined to try and prevent it in the future. Yet uttering 'the oldest profession' is expected to induce resignation towards the existence of the sex trade because, well, it's been going on *ages*. In 2014 media sharing site Upworthy, which says its mission is to draw 'massive amounts of attention to things that matter',[11] posted a link on its Facebook page to an infographic about the sex trade with this introduction: 'It's the world's oldest profession, so I'm sure it's not going anywhere anytime soon. And I can only imagine it's not an easy way to make a living, so why make it any harder?'[12] (At the time of writing, the company's Facebook page has 7.7 million 'likes'.)[13] Underneath the infographic Upworthy then links to an article that begins, 'There's no way to end demand for sex work.'[14] And in case readers still hadn't got the message, the photo immediately below is captioned, 'The world's oldest profession isn't going anywhere.'

'The oldest profession' is not a description, it's prostitution's unofficial brand; encouraging people to feel relaxed about the sex trade, unconcerned by its existence, helpless even if they aren't.

Crucially, the myth that the sex trade is inevitable has long obscured the choices of the men who decide to become its 'consumers'. The implication is that either these buyers can't help themselves or, accepting they can, it wouldn't make much difference anyway because the sex trade is always going to exist. Because, well, *because*. So when the public gaze falls on the trade, it is as though a spotlight is pointed straight at the women whose bodies constitute its raw material. The attentions of commentators and policy makers revolve around them in a tightly lit political space, their actions endlessly scrutinised. Yet rarely is the assessor's field of vision wide enough to take in anyone else present in the scene. When explanations and recommendations are doled out, it's as if this trade uniquely, and impossibly, begins and ends with *supply*.

This isn't a recent trend. In 1893 the aforementioned Italian criminologist Cesare Lombroso concluded that the cause of prostitution lay with women. He claimed he had proof that women in prostitution have smaller brains than other women, heavier lower jaws, a 'masculine larynx', bigger calves, and that they were more likely to have hairy moles (which Lombroso believed 'must be added to the signs of degeneration in women').[15] He was joined in 1936 by Danish geneticist Dr Tage Kemp, who announced he had uncovered evidence of the sex trade's origins in the bodies of 530 women. Kemp, who would later become director of the University Institute of Human Genetics in Copenhagen, reported, 'hereditary taint is widespread among prostitutes. In many cases it should be regarded as one of the most important causal factors – indeed, frequently as the actual cause of prostitution.'[16] Yet while researchers were busy trying to formulate a diagnosis for prostitution by measuring women's bones and counting their hairs, the 'health' of the men who paid women for sex was not subject to similar scrutiny.

This pathologising of women involved in the sex trade is now roundly recognised for the pernicious quackery it is. Nonetheless, its spirit is still invoked on occasion, like when Dennis Hof, owner of the Moonlite BunnyRanch brothel in Nevada, told a journalist: 'Bunnies don't say no. Very seldom. I mean, all girls have their limits, but the bunny girls have higher limits. And so typically they don't say no.'[17] While the notion that the sex trade is 'caused' by the (albeit curtailed) choices of women was made explicit by researchers like Kemp, today the notion is largely peddled implicitly, but no less determinedly. The driving force that is *demand* remains hidden from view.

As the economist John Maynard Keynes pointed out, 'All production is for the purpose of ultimately satisfying a consumer.'[18] The desire and willingness of some men to pay to sexually access women's bodies is the primary foundation on which strip clubs, porn sets and brothels around the world are built. The notion that the choices of these men are somehow irrelevant or peripheral to the existence of the sex industry is absurd. If the demand didn't exist, the trade would collapse.

So what are the reasons some men demand the sex trade – and what does the trade demand of them?

This is a classic case of 'the pretty ones don't have to work hard'. Vicky is beautiful, but frankly can't be arsed. She's Polish, and her English is not good . . . I was reminded of the Smiths' song 'Girlfriend in a Coma' . . . All the while she seemed completely disinterested and mechanical . . . After a while, during which she remained completely unresponsive, I offered to lick her – she was stubbly, which I dislike, but carried on regardless, and got the same lack of response . . . I finally decided to fuck her, in mish. Her pussy was hot and tight, and I came after less than ten minutes. All the while, she kept her face turned to one side.

Sex buyer online review[19]

Amount paid: £100

Prostitution

The proportion of men who 'demand' the prostitution trade varies between countries. In Australia, 15.6 per cent of men have paid for sex,[20] in the USA 14 per cent have,[21] while in

Ireland the figure is 8 per cent.[22] Showing just how variable rates can be, surveys carried out in the UK a decade apart found that the rate of men reporting having paid for sex nearly doubled during the 1990s.[23] The proportion soared from one in twenty men to almost one in ten.

Interviews with 137 sex buyers by the Child and Woman Abuse Studies Unit at London Metropolitan University found that over half of the men were either married or in a relationship, over a fifth had children, and nearly 90 per cent were in paid employment.[24] A five-country research programme led by the Immigrant Council of Ireland showed that the majority of men who have paid for sex don't do it frequently,[25] while a study of 103 London-based sex buyers uncovered that over three-quarters of the men had already paid for sex by the time they were twenty-five years old.[26] Contrary to portrayals of the sex trade as a place of last resort for men otherwise unable to find a sexual partner, a survey of 6000 UK men (one in ten of whom had paid for sex) found that those most likely to have paid for sex were young professionals with high numbers of sexual partners.[27] On average, sex buyers had over double the number of sexual partners than men who had not paid for sex.[28]

While research reveals significant demographic diversity among men who pay for sex, commonality is clear in the attitudes and beliefs that underpin why they do it, what they feel entitled to get for their money, and how they justify it. Evidence of these attitudes is not hard to come by. The notion that the demand propping up the prostitution trade has been ignored for so long because it is difficult to research the secretive world of sex buyers is quickly quashed when you actually try and do it. I placed a small advert in a local newspaper, asking men who paid for sex to contact me to share their views, and my phone practically rang off the hook.

I heard an assortment of explanations when I asked the men who responded to my ad why they paid women for sex: 'I like the excitement, the variety'; 'I don't have any option . . . At the moment I'm just single so I have to buy it'; 'It's just a male thing where it's get as many as you can . . . It's not a fact of what do you like about it, you don't actually like it. I think it's just a fact of "I've done my duty and that's it, I'm off".'

For one of the men I spoke to, revenge was a spur: 'I think it's if you get pissed off with your missus to be quite honest, a lot of the time.' Another insisted that paying women for sex was no different from a regular relationship.

When I was married, if my wife wanted a new dress, new crockery, went out on a holiday, took her for a meal, I knew I'd always get the sex. It was in the same perspective. I pay for it. I didn't always look for it. Sometimes she would give it to me freely without, whatever. But honestly, no different. When a man marries a woman, he comes into a contract with her. And in that contract is [conjugal] rights to sexual gratification and also for the bearing of children.

It would be tempting to dismiss a view like this as the bitter ramblings of a lone knuckle-dragger; rather less easy to do when you consider that mainstream lads' mag *FHM* ran a feature in its UK edition asking, 'How much are you paying for sex?' A form helped readers calculate their 'pay per lay'.[29] This involved totting up expenditure on outgoings like flowers and dividing it by the number of times they had sex with their partner that month. If it 'cost' the reader less than £5 to have sex, *FHM* advised him it was 'too cheap – she's about the same price as a Cambodian whore'.

While the casual explanations offered by punters vary, a recurring theme binds them together. Studies of men who pay for sex confirm what was abundantly clear in my interviews: sex buyers feel *entitled*.[30] They feel entitled to pay women to perform sex acts on them because they 'want to', 'need to'; empowered by the belief that men's prostitution of women is inevitable and acceptable. For Crystal, who was first coerced into prostitution by her abusive boyfriend, it essentially boils down to the fact that 'they know they can get away with it, that they can remain in the shadows and if anyone is judged it will be the woman'.

A good service

What I found particularly shocking when interviewing sex buyers was how unabashedly some of them spoke of having sex with women they knew didn't want to have it with them. Having handed over money, punters typically demand more than just sexual access to a woman's body. They demand a 'good service' (as one man put it). What qualifies as a good service was neatly and chillingly summed up by one of my interviewees: 'Obviously it's my money. I want them to treat me the way I want, and not the way they want.'

Professor Donna M. Hughes, a leading US scholar on human trafficking, studied online 'reviews' of women posted by men who had paid them for sex acts. 'They have "good" experiences when women comply with everything the men want them to do, focus all their attention on the men, and pretend they like the men and enjoy the sex acts . . . Men have "bad" experiences when women will not do everything they want, or are disinterested, perfunctory, and try to minimize the physical contact with them.'[31]

One of the sex buyers I spoke to complained about an occasion he paid a woman for sex but she 'didn't seem up for it at all'. He described having sex with a woman who obviously didn't want to be having sex with him as a 'very bad service, very'. He recalled to me over the phone,

It was a house I went in and seemed like a secretary or someone answered the door. There was a pick of two girls and obviously I went for the most gorgeous one . . . We went upstairs and, how can I say, she was, like, very frigid. Very frigid. It was very disappointing in the sense I was paying . . . If I went to suck her breasts she was like, 'Oh no, no, no.' If I went and put my hand down there she's like, 'Oh, no, no, no, no, no.' Really, really crap like that. Even [when] she was giving a massage, hand relief – no touching in places like I would like. Even the sex was really, really crap. It was really, really disappointing.

Another disgruntled sex buyer told me, 'Some I've had have been pretty poor value for money so I've disliked that.' I asked the man what he deemed to be poor value for money. 'Them clearly not enjoying it. Them being disrespectful and just rushing through it. You know, 'cause they're just going to do the bare minimum, get the money and that's that. Others pretend to enjoy it because they're smart business women.' Crystal told me how she abhorred this requirement by sex buyers that she pretend to want everything they want and like everything they like.

> I scorned them for their pathetic egos, for choosing to pretend I wanted to be there and was enjoying what they did when it was obvious I was in a real mess – reeking of booze or out of it, bruises. They would sometimes tell me about their wives or girlfriends and how boring they were sexually in comparison to me. I wanted to say, 'What you're doing is painful not fun. No wonder she says no to you.'

One man actually mused about the experiences of abuse and disadvantage that might have led to the women he paid finding themselves in a room with him. 'I really feel for them,' he said. 'I think, "Poor girls, I wonder what life they have lived and it's come down to this" . . . It must be very hard for them when they get customers come through who are maybe unhygienic or just really dog rough ugly or they're just giving them orders and stuff . . . What they're doing is very, very, very tough for them, you know. You should take a moment just to think, why have they come to that?' Indeed. UK research analysing women's experiences of prostitution has found that approximately 50 per cent of women became involved before their eighteenth birthday;[32] up to 95 per cent of women in street prostitution are problematic drug users,[33] and over 50 per cent have been raped and/or sexually assaulted, mostly by sex buyers.[34] Women in prostitution are also almost eighteen times more likely to be murdered than women not involved in the trade.[35] And yet the experiences of trauma and neglect suspected by the man I was speaking to, which made him 'really feel' for the women, didn't put him off. After telling me of his apparently heartfelt concerns, he casually explained that when paying for sex he still expected a 'good service', which meant, 'You know, she has to be friendly. She has to be looking like she's up for it as well, not looking like she can't be bothered. She's got to have a service, she's got to sell it to her customer, make him feel good, relaxed, chilled out. Make him feel horny.'

This active disinterest among sex buyers in hearing how the woman being paid really feels extends to how she got there in the first place. In-depth interviews with sex buyers in Lithuania and Bulgaria revealed that the possibility a woman might have been trafficked was unlikely to be a consideration when handing over money for sexual access to her, regardless of how aware the man was of trafficking in general.[36] And of 202 sex buyers interviewed by researchers in Boston, 41 per cent said they knew that women they had paid for sex were under the control of a pimp.[37]

'Sex tourism' can offer a clear view of how the demands made by some sex buyers are infused with racism and exploit power differentials along multiple fronts. One online forum dedicated to this particular subset of buyers declared,

Women in Western countries are spoiled bitches . . . But there are many places in the world where women will treat you like a king for a minor fraction of what your Western girlfriend costs. Any woman living outside of the Western world knows that if she treats her man poorly he will walk down the street and have her replaced in less than fifteen minutes. Accordingly, when you tell your non-Western girlfriend to start sucking she knows she better do a real good job! This website is about finding those types of women. [38]

In an analysis of discussions taking place on the ClubHombre website among sex buyers visiting Tijuana, Mexico, researcher Yasmina Katsulis found that most of the men were white, lived in southern California, and half reported earning over $85,000 (US) a year. Racial stereotypes about Mexican women abounded in their posts, with men seeking out a fantasy of a 'traditional' woman. Katsulis observed, 'Mexicanas are repeatedly portrayed as more open-minded and accepting, and a preference for the intrinsic asymmetry in the relationship is legitimated and naturalized.'[39]

A sizeable portion of men who pay for sex acknowledge that prostitution is harmful to women:

- 39 per cent of sex buyers interviewed by researchers in Scotland agreed that prostitution is a form of sexual exploitation, while 85 per cent believed that women involved don't enjoy the sex of prostitution.[40]
- 42 per cent of punters in a Chicago-based study thought prostitution caused physical and psychological damage to those selling sex and 32 per cent believed that the majority of women in prostitution became involved as children.[41]
- 44 per cent of sex buyers taking part in a London-based study felt prostitution has a very or extremely negative impact on women involved.[42]

So how to square all this? While openly acknowledging prostitution is harmful to women involved, how can a sex buyer simultaneously feel entitled to demand a 'good service' from them? In essence, how can he live with himself?

The self-soothing properties of myths

Listening to punters' linguistic and cognitive contortions when justifying paying for sex is to be given a textbook case study in the strategies psychologist Albert Bandura found people use to disengage their own ethics.* Bandura's theory is that people adopt 'standards of right and wrong that serve

* Bandura's theory has previously been brilliantly applied by philosopher Dr Rebecca Whisnant to pornography consumption in her essay, 'From Jekyll to Hyde: the grooming of male pornography consumers'.[43]

as guides and deterrents for conduct'.[44] These standards for how to treat other people become part of our identity, part of our sense of self, and regulate our behaviour. However, there are ways of muting this inner ethical voice. 'Psycho-social manoeuvres' can work to muffle it, freeing the person to commit inhumane acts. Manoeuvres like reframing harmful action as a social good ('I would describe prostitution as [a] service to the community,' one sex buyer told me) and using euphemisms to make the action seem more palatable (it's just a 'business matter', another maintained).

It is also a whole lot easier to snuff out the self-sanctioning effects of empathy when you view your target as sub-human, as an object. Sex buyers piece together a kind of cognitive flak jacket from these strategies to protect against condemnation from themselves and others. It is also adopted by the body politic at times, with john-justifying fantasies like 'it is the oldest game' (as one sex buyer 'reminded' me) rolled out as reasons to accept the trade. As Bandura makes clear, the power of these justifications should not be underestimated: 'It requires conducive social conditions rather than monstrous people to produce atrocious deeds. Given appropriate social conditions, decent, ordinary people can do extraordinarily cruel things.' [45] It takes myths, not monsters.

When I asked a sex buyer I was interviewing where control sits in the act of prostitution, he snapped back without hesitation, 'Obviously the man. Because he's paying for it, he is the boss.' According to Crystal, he pretty much nailed it.

The closest they ever came to asking how I felt would be telling me 'You love that don't you' – a statement not a question. I guess the closest they came to asking what I wanted was asking what 'services' I performed, so they knew what they owed me (different things cost extra). Because the johns have all the power, there is no real honest communication and no mutuality. You are the goods he's paid for, expected to deliver not just physically but in terms of cleanliness, make-up, lingerie, dirty talk and a smile all packaged pretty to massage his ego and make him feel he's got his money's worth.

In paying a person to have sex with him, the punter purchases control and buys off mutuality. He may request a 'girlfriend experience', and even pay extra for the privilege, but as US researchers noted of some of the sex buyers who were interviewed as part of a Boston-based study, they wanted women to act like girlfriends with 'no feelings who made no demands on them and who would automatically be aroused by every sex act they demanded'.[46]

A minority of men currently demand prostitution, but prostitution demands something of them too. They have to be proficient in viewing women as dehumanised sexual objects. It is a prerequisite for a man actually being able to stand having sex with a woman who doesn't freely want to have it with him, let alone desiring this and forking out for the privilege. In paying for sex, not only do punters deem consideration of the genuine feelings and wants of women they are paying a trifling irrelevance to the act, many require the performance of the brutal charade that they don't even possess these basic human faculties. One of my interviewees insisted, 'She should at least give the impression that she's enjoying what she's doing because it's better customer service. She should be smart enough to make us want to come back and do this.' In this, the sex buyer demands that the person he is paying enthusiastically embraces the subservient status of sexual object he has assigned to them; he requires they work hard to ensure something pesky like basic human empathy doesn't interfere with his arousal.

Saw this girl's pictures on the other site and thought she looked nice. How wrong I was. She does NOT offer any of the services offered and actually had the cheek to ask for more money to perform things that she is advertising as part of her services!! Her attitude was derisory . . . I did have sex with her which was a bit like shagging a blow up doll. I should have asked for my money back but given the very dodgy looking bloke with a very aggressive dog downstairs I thought it best to just get out as fast as possible.

Sex buyer online review[47]

Amount paid: £60

Lap-dancing clubs

The strip-club industry underwent something of a financial revolution during the 1980s. The phenomenon of men paying women to perform for their sexual gratification, irrespective of hers, goes much further back, of course. But during this period the business model servicing this demand underwent some game-changing adjustments. Out went actually hiring women to perform in the clubs and in came self-employed 'independent contractors', required to pay a kind of rent for space in the club. (Though as Sandrine Levêque, former campaigner at women's rights group Object, points out, despite ostensibly being self-employed, performers would nonetheless be 'bound by fines or dismissal to a variety of rules and customs'.[48]) The lucrative trend of 'lap dancing' was added to the menus of many clubs. For punters, this was an opportunity to pay for a one-on-one private striptease with bodily contact; for performers, it was now one of the few ways they could actually make any money in the club. The strip-club shop front also got a makeover. 'Gentlemen's club' became the key brand concept, rolled out to update the clubs' public image from seedy to sophisticated. Punters would be required to help keep up appearances by adhering to a dress code befitting of such a clientele.

Sandrine and I met in 2007 while campaigning to change the licensing laws regulating lap-dancing clubs in the UK. One of the (intended) consequences of the strip-club rebrand was to help move strip clubs from the back street to the high street; changing perceptions of the clubs, not only among the general public but among the officials handing out licences for premises. Hence the Lap Dancing Association (LDA), a group of club owners who came together to (unsuccessfully) oppose Object and the Fawcett Society's campaign to tighten up licensing laws, argued that, 'Lap-dancing clubs are a small part of the vibrant UK leisure and entertainment industry.' While lap dancing is 'a sexy industry', they claimed, it shouldn't be mistaken for being part of the 'sex industry'.[49]

Fantastical as the LDA's claim was, the message that lap-dancing clubs are part of the mainstream leisure industry gained traction and, paired with a reworked business model, helped lay the foundations for a strip club boom. The UK's first lap-dancing club opened in 1995. Assisted by lax licensing laws, the number doubled to over 300 clubs between 2004 and 2008 alone.[50] But licensing regulations and strategic branding don't explain the basic matter of why lap-dancing clubs are able to turn a profit. They don't explain why some men want to visit clubs where they select women and pay them to strip.

The attraction

For Lucy, who used to work in lap-dancing clubs in London, the suggestion that the appeal for punters lies purely and simply in the sexual pleasure of seeing a woman remove her clothes doesn't even begin to cover it. She told me how the men who paid her would also 'enjoy the transaction':

They enjoy the idea of giving money for this thing. I think because it enforces their idea that they are more powerful and that they should be more powerful and that this is a place – at last – in this whole society that no longer allows them to feel this way. Here is a haven where 'I'm a man and I can pay you to do this thing and you think I'm great.' You know, 'Just come over to my table and express how great you think I am. And now you're taking your clothes off for me . . . And it doesn't matter that I'm not attractive to you really. It doesn't matter that if we were in a pub this would never happen, because here it is happening.'

A visitor to Peter Stringfellow's club in London enthused about this altered reality in an online review of his visit: 'The women make you feel like a king,' he wrote.[51] Strip clubs don't exist to provide necessary release for 'uncontrollable urges'. They offer men the chance to acquire control. 'You wouldn't just be on offer to everyone in a normal situation,' Lucy explained. 'They wouldn't just have the power to choose.'

Jennifer Danns performed in a lap-dancing club in the north of England during her early twenties. Her assessment of what lap-dancing clubs offer men who visit echoes Lucy's. 'It can be very difficult to get a customer to accept a dance from you,' Jennifer told me. 'There are often over thirty women, certainly more in larger clubs, competing for the same customers, and the man has the power to choose whoever he wants. And he knows it.' A patron of Larry Flynt's Hustler

Club wrote excitedly about this in his online review: 'Hot women from all over Europe gives you the chance to choose what you like, almost like a sexy version of a pick-and-mix!'[52] Jennifer remembers how this process of selection could become increasingly distressing as the shift wore on. As the men 'are approached by more and more girls, their ego becomes inflated'.

> They can reject you in very hurtful ways . . . I would have men tell me to my face that they didn't like black girls, my tits were too small, too big. I wasn't thin enough. I once had one man who saw me exit the bathroom and said to me that he was going to ask me for a dance but now he knows I have used the toilet I have put him right off, because of course lap dancers don't burp, fart, go to the toilet or do anything other than perform lap dances like a machine.

The sexual politics described by Lucy and Jennifer were evident in a US study of regular strip-club users by a researcher at the University of Wisconsin. Many of the men felt relations between women and men in everyday life were 'tense' or 'confused'.[53] Visiting a lap-dancing club offered some welcome respite. 'With all of this sexual harassment stuff going around these days, men need somewhere to go where they can say and act like they want,' insisted one of the men. These strategic retreats from the scary new frontiers of feminism constitute what academics have dubbed 'masculinising practices'.

As another punter explained, having visited strip clubs while his marriage was on the rocks, strip clubs were 'good for my ego, to build me up, to make me feel like I was a man again'. The fact that strip-club users can 'man up' in the presence of other men is far from incidental either. Punters provide an audience on two fronts: for performers and for each other. 'Proving' masculinity is, as sociologist Dr Michael Flood puts it, 'a homosocial enactment, in which the performance of manhood is in front of, and granted by, other men'.[54]

Lucy noticed, however, that not all of the men who visited the clubs where she worked were equally thrilled at the prospect: 'I think a lot of them just go because they just don't want to say no. They think they're meant to enjoy it. Lots of the ones that go, go anyway even though they don't enjoy it.' But reluctant or not, they would still assume the role of clothed observer and pay women to strip naked for them. 'Even the men who think that they're different or think that they're being nice or think that they're able to treat you like a human being, aren't.' Jennifer remembered how on occasion punters would balk at the prospect of a one-on-one lap dance. 'A group of men would enter the club and most of the group would pay for a private dance. One member of the group would sit quietly and eventually one of his friends would pay for him to have a private dance.' Once he and Jennifer had entered the private room 'he would ask me to stay clothed and just sit with him. After enough time had passed he would beg me to not mention to his friends what had happened and please pretend that he had had a topless dance.'

Do's and don'ts

The degree of mainstream acceptability lap-dancing clubs have acquired means owners can now boast that their venues are a regular stop-off on the stag do route. The Stag Company, which bills itself as 'the world's biggest hen and stag company', informs stag do planners on its website that 'the lovely Peter Stringfellow made lap dancing a popular recreational activity for the British male population and when planning a stag weekend the first thing that's added to the list is lap dancing'.[55] Despite the veneer of normality surrounding lap-dancing clubs, The Stag Company feels it necessary to include a word of advice for prospective visitors on how to behave in the clubs: 'Remember that you cannot touch even though you think you have special privileges because you are on your stag night.' The reason? Apparently not because touching without consent would in fact constitute sexual assault, but because 'Barry the Bouncer might frog march you 'otta [sic] there.'

The reality, however, is that 'Barry the Bouncer' isn't always able to keep a lid on violence against women in the clubs. Kelly Holsopple was inspired to conduct research into women's experiences of strip clubs having been a performer herself for thirteen years. Of the women she questioned, 100 per cent had been subjected to sexual, physical and verbal abuse – mostly by punters.[56] 'Customers often attempt and succeed at penetrating strippers vaginally and anally with their fingers, dollar bills, and bottles', Holsopple reported. 'Customers ex-

pose their penises, rub their penises on women, and mastur-
bate in front of the women.' Hardly any of the men who
committed these assaults faced any consequences. Holsopple
described sexual violence in strip clubs as 'institutionalised',
'normalized' and 'socially sanctioned'. Similarly, when another US researcher investigated women's experiences in strip
clubs she discovered that each of the performers interviewed
recalled punters who had 'touched her in offensive ways'.

> They all have had men kiss them, without their consent,
> while working. One dancer complained about a client
> who shoved his tongue down her throat, another
> informant described an incident in which a customer put
> his tongue inside her vagina when she was performing
> a naked dance, and another quit stripping after a client
> stuck three fingers inside her vagina. [57]

Lap-dancing clubs are venues dedicated to the act of sexually objectifying women. The enthusiasm shown by men
paying to enter these shrines to sexism varies, from those
just tagging along to those who relish embracing the sov-
ereign sexual control of someone made to feel 'like a king'.
But all opt to enter a venue in which he is made subject and
she is made object. Where her designated role is to sexually
satisfy him, at his bidding. It was this dehumanising act of
objectification that Lucy found to be the most pernicious
part of performing in lap-dancing clubs: 'You feel somewhere inside you that you should be reciprocated. You feel

like it should matter to them whether or not that you fancy them. But you realise that it doesn't.' And when the entire set-up of the clubs hinges on punters not caring whether their sexual desire for a woman is reciprocated, it makes sense that companies organising visits to lap-dancing clubs may feel it necessary to remind customers not to commit sexual assault.

Very pretty and young girl. Approximately 165cm tall, nice legs and beautiful breast, nice skin. Very young . . . If you want to try a fresh, young (says she is 18) and pretty girl is ok, but maybe as she just started to work, is quite passive, scarcely kiss without tongue, doesn't want to be kissed on the neck or ears, can't do a decent blowjob and really rides badly on you, i had to stop her several times when she tried to use her mouth or when she got up on me. She really can't speak a work of english (is romenian) so even gfe* is a zero.

Sex buyer online review[58]

Amount paid: £70

*gfe = 'girlfriend experience'

Pornography

Why do men demand porn? It's a question that could seem unworthy of an answer, appearing both obvious and obsolete. That porn producers are responding to clickers' curiosity and search for sexual pleasure is hardly revelatory stuff. It is also the arm of the sex trade that can claim the most women among its 'demand', prompting suggestions that the more relevant question is, 'Why do *people* demand porn?' Yet in spite of the commercial compulsion to crack open under-exploited markets, porn profiteers have barely been able to scratch the surface of the female 'consumer base'. And convenient as it would be for porn industry lobbyists to shake off the industry's sexist reputation with a hat-tip to women's insatiable demand for it, they can't. (Or at least, they can't do it honestly.)

Analyses of porn consumption have repeatedly demonstrated that when it comes to seeking out pornography, men are more likely than women to (a) do it, (b) do it repeatedly, (c) do it to get turned on, (d) do it and feel turned on, and (e) do it and still think porn is a good thing afterwards.[59] Gender differences are there from the get-go. A 2013 survey by the University of East London found that the vast majority of twelve- to sixteen-year-old boys had watched online porn, while only a minority of girls had.[60] Digging beneath this top-line finding, researchers also uncovered a gender divide in how young people were 'engaging' with pornography. Girls tended to take a look via social media sites while in a group, and were substantially more likely to feel 'confused, angry or frightened' by it. Boys, on the other hand, mostly watched porn on their own. The pornography industry is driven by the demand from its biggest consumer group: heterosexual men. So the question of why these men demand pornography is not obsolete, it's central.

However, that still leaves charges of the bleeding obvious hanging over the question of why so many men demand pornography. Industry cheerleader and former owner of Britain's biggest porn site, Jerry Barnett, claims in defence of the product he helps peddle that it is merely 'sexual and erotic expression'.[61] Accepting Barnett's premise, the logic unfolds thus: sex is natural, porn is sex, ergo, porn is natural. Inevitable. Those who oppose the trade, he claims, are 'anti-sex'. This is, of course, mud that has been relentlessly hurled over successive decades in the direction of anyone with the audacity to critique the business of porn. Evidently Barnett is still optimistic about its ability to stick. (More on that later.) The implication is that the demand oiling the wheels of the pornography trade is simply sexual desire.

But it all gets rather more complicated when you consider what is actually being demanded.

The medium

First the medium of the product. The footage churned out by the pornography industry is filmed prostitution. Pornography is not a synonym for sex. Needless to say, Los Angeles's porn producers are not intrepid ethnographers. They do not spend long days pacing around local neighbourhoods, patiently waiting to hear the muffled tones of people locked in the throes of ecstasy. At which point, they do not burst in, wave a contract in the lucky couple's faces, proceed to set up their filming equipment and, having been given the OK by the surprised but remarkably relaxed film subjects, simply allow them to carry on having sex as they were. Porn production companies pay the women who appear in their films to turn up to a designated place at a designated time to have sex in a designated way with a designated person. Country-specific studies suggest most men who watch pornography won't have visited a brothel or picked up a woman on the street, and many would deem the very idea of prostitution as sexist and degrading. Yet in consuming porn, they are seeking sexual gratification from watching filmed footage of it.

The extra twist is that in much heterosexual porn, as opposed to 'traditional' prostitution, women are paid to have sex with men who are also being paid. Feminist philosopher Rebecca Whisnant points out that this doesn't alter the fundamental set-up. 'So essentially, a male prostitute has entered the scene and is now participating alongside the female prostitute. But what of it? The basic structure of pimp, prostitute and customer [producers, performer and porn user] remains intact . . . the transaction has simply become immensely more profitable for the pimp.'[62]

Of course, on top of this framework there are distinct dynamics at play in what is traditionally divided up as prostitution and porn production, which could colour the experience of the person being paid to have sex. In 'standard' prostitution, for instance, the sex buyer is usually completely unknown, hasn't signed a contract through which he could conceivably be traced, and is suitably motivated to pay for a woman to sexually 'service' him – and all the expectations of a 'good service' which go along with that. On the other hand, participating in standard porn production will mean the sex acts a woman is paid to perform will be permanently documented, publicly accessible and viewed by an untold number of people. And while the man or men she is having sex with are also there on the condition of being paid, any conceivable motivation he may be lacking in extracting what's deemed a 'good service' from her will be more than made up for in the director, producer, distributor, agent, and so on. Besides, any lines it's possible to draw between these two 'commercial sex' scenarios are frequently blurred, and sometimes erased altogether, as I'll show.

The fact that the footage churned out by porn production companies is a choreographed form of prostitution is not some incidental academic footnote. Commercial dynamics are utterly pivotal to what porn users see and performers experience. Jessie first set foot on a porn set the day after her eighteenth birthday. 'I actually spoke to an agent when I was seventeen and everything was coordinated for all my shoots, to go after I turned eighteen.' I spoke to Jessie a year after she got out of the industry, but she still remembered her first day and how dizzyingly quickly her preconceptions about the trade were blown apart. At her first meeting with an industry agent, Jessie was given a document that listed different sex acts and scenarios. The agent 'asked me to circle what I was OK with doing and initially I only circled *solo*, which is like basically just nude shots of me fondling myself'. But the agent made clear her disappointment. 'She was like, "Well, you know, with just doing this you're not going to make as much money as I proposed to you."' The pressure to 'do more' escalated. 'A lot of people tried pushing me to do anal. I kept saying no.' But not long after starting out, an experience on set changed everything.

'I was shooting all day,' remembers Jessie. 'It was before I got my breast augmentation actually, and I was only shooting with another girl and I was also doing solo work. And so I thought everything would be very soft, not hardcore.' It turned out that wasn't what the director had in mind. 'He had me do a lot of weird things, like sticking a broom inside of myself and stuff like that.' And towards the end of the session he asked Jessie 'to stick a speculum inside of my vagina. And I told him no. I had already shot all day, it was night-time already.' The director's response? 'He said, "Well, I'm not going to give you your cheque if you don't do this." And I was like, "Oh, oh my god. Like, what am I going to do?" I'm not even OK with a gynaecologist doing that, like, I have a weird phobia of those things. And he wanted to open it, like, wide.'

Jessie had wound up performing in pornography after struggling to make ends meet with two minimum wage jobs, waiting tables at Hooters and modelling for a clothes shop. Searching on the website Craigslist she spotted a job ad that read in capital letters, MAKE $20,000–30,000 A MONTH

MODELLING. 'I was like, "Oh this looks interesting, like, I had done regular modelling before",' Jessie remembers. But it was only when she was sitting in the office of the company that had placed the ad that Jessie was actually told the job would be having sex on camera. 'Everything people told me, they would say, "Oh, well, you get treated like a princess and you make all this money" and "You make more money than the male performer and because of that it's empowering", and stuff like that . . . that was always what I envisioned it to be.'

Yet here was Jessie on set being told she wouldn't get paid unless she let a speculum be inserted into her vagina.

So I decided to go through with it. And the whole time he was filming I was crying the whole time. It was very, very, very painful. He was just like, 'Oh you're OK, you're OK', whatever. And then when we were done with that I was still trying to gather myself, the girl that was there with me she was like, 'Yeah, it's OK.' She was like, 'It's happened to all of us.'

But the shoot wasn't over yet.

I had another scene to do for him and I was, like, I don't know how I'm going to do this, like, my vagina was hurting really bad. And basically I decided to stick a toy up my butt instead, and in a weird way it was kind of like a relief to me that I could, you know, have that kind of alternative because my vagina was just hurting really bad. And from that point on I kind of realised that for me to survive in the industry I would have to do anal so my pussy wouldn't get so tore up.

The commercial set-up of pornography meant that despite being clear and explicit at the outset about what she would and wouldn't do, Jessie was heavily pressured to take part in painful, unwanted sex acts.

While publicly the porn industry likes to steer clear of the suggestion that it is a highly lucrative prostitution racket, Jessie's experiences suggest efforts behind the scenes to hive off pornography from the sex trade's other outputs are rather more relaxed. 'My agent actually tried getting me involved with webcamming as well,' Jessie recalls, 'but I didn't like that very much. There's other agents that book girls for – they call it feature dancing but that's just a fancy word for stripping. And there's some agents that also book girls for escorting. So they do everything. It's always like this cycle of stripping, porn, webcamming, escorting.' The distinctions dissolve even further in the trend known as 'fan porn'.[63] In these types of porn films, women are paid to have sex with regular porn users. So the viewer is no longer vicariously participating in prostitution; he has become the john.

The message

Profit margins not only underpin the fundamental dynamics of porn production, they also dictate trends in the content churned out by producers. They dictate the message. US researcher Ana Bridges conducted a ground-breaking analysis of pornography content which highlighted two key forces driving industry trends: competition and habituation. In a consumer space now awash with pornography, and technological developments making it easier and cheaper than ever before to film and distribute it, producers are being pushed to find a USP. They have to find a way to elbow their porn to the front of the crowd. There is also evidence suggesting porn profiteers are simultaneously waging a battle with boredom. A shocking event or image feels progressively less shocking as time passes and as a person is repeatedly exposed to it. This psychological process of habituation presents a challenge for porn producers. 'Studies of men viewing sexually explicit movies have demonstrated that habituation occurs over time such that sexual arousal (as measured by penile tumescence) decreases with repeated viewing of the same film,' Bridges writes.[64] If more of the same won't cut it for consumers, porn profiteers will seek out the novel.

Yet porn viewers aren't just (perhaps unwittingly) demanding the industry pursue the new. One trend above all others has come to define the business of porn: violence and aggression. There is a fair degree of openness about this among industry insiders. Back in 2003, the pornography trade bible, *Adult Video News*, featured a cover story headlined, 'Harder, faster: can porn get any nastier?'[65] The editor wrote, 'There's no question there's been a turn for the harder in the XXX in recent years. In the mid-1990s, double penetration seemed to be the bar for nasty. Then came the massive gangbangs, such as Houston 620 in 1999, bukkake vids (also 1999) and today . . . throat fucking, ass-to-mouth, double-vaginal and double-anal penetration is [*sic*] not uncommon.'

When Jessie started out in the industry, she remembers watching porn 'to see, you know, what other people did and what else was out there. I saw these websites of girls getting hung upside down and just a ton of crazy stuff and I was like, "Oh I don't know if I would ever do that. I don't think I would." And sure enough I ended up doing everything.' Jessie reeled off to me the types of porn films she ended up appearing in, despite initially telling her agent she only wanted to do 'solo': 'I did gonzo porn – which is just like non-scripted internet stuff. I did the feature films, which is like, all day shooting . . . I did live shows. I did solos. I did public stuff . . . I worked with several men at once, so I've done gang bangs. I did BDSM.' She then mentioned, matter-of-factly, 'I've also done electricity [porn] where I've been electrocuted . . . Basically, anything you can think of.' I asked Jessie how it all affected her at the time. 'In the very beginning I would go home and cry,' she replied. 'But then there was a point in time where I said I need to toughen up and just make this money and whatever. And so I started drinking more.'

Violent and aggressive pornography is not some small-scale fad on the industry's fringes. A study published in 2010 by Ana Bridges and colleagues analysed the top-selling porn films, as tracked by *Adult Video News*, over a period of six months.[66] They found 88 per cent of scenes featured physical aggression

– such as slapping, hair pulling, choking and gagging (defined as 'when an object or body part, e.g., penis, hand, or sex toy, is inserted into a character's mouth, visibly obstructing breathing'). 94 per cent of all the physical and verbal aggression was directed at women. The researchers also found 41 per cent of scenes contained an act called 'ass-to-mouth'. It's pretty much as the name suggests: a male performer inserts his penis into a woman's anus and then immediately afterwards puts it into her or another woman's mouth. Analysing porn film reviews published in *Adult Video News,* sociologist Dr Meagan Tyler also found that 'extreme, violent or degrading acts' were often highlighted for their profit potential. [67] As one reviewer enthused about a film: 'Finally, Julie Night gets analized [*sic*] by dildos, buttplugs and three guys, with more d.p. and double anal – and in the finale, Nicki spoons cum from Julie's ass to her mouth! Now, that's pornography!'

The choreographed prostitution of mainstream heterosexual pornography is saturated with cruelty and contempt towards the women in it. This escalates the question of why so many men demand it to *how* could so many men demand it? How could so many men not only choose to sit through footage of women being choked, gagged, hit and humiliated during sex, but also gain sexual pleasure from this?

The answer is: only with the help of some deeply manipulating tactics by pornographers. The wider culture in which porn consumers live is riddled with gender inequality, both feeding and feeding off the sexual objectification of women. The profits for pornographers lie in further mining this misogyny to make viewers feel like 'a real man'. And yet, while doing this, directors have to take care not to inadvertently tap into the consumer's empathy. In an online forum discussing the question, 'When watching porn, what is an instant boner killer?', the nearly 3,000 replies (at the time of writing) included unremarkable statements like, 'When the guy is chewing gum loudly at the camera' and 'When it stops to load'.[68] Others, however, mentioned that seeing the consequences of violence against women took a toll on their erection: 'Vocaliztions that sound painful'; 'When the girl gives the camera a dead-eyed stare or doesn't look like she's enjoying herself'; 'Angry porn where the actress is practically crying, instant boner killer'; 'Gaping buttholes. I'm all for anal sex, but when women in porn have those gaping buttholes that allow you to pretty much look into their stomachs it is an instant boner killer for me.'

The trick for pornographers, then, is to get the right *balance* of sexism. Porn producers have an array of devices up their sleeves to achieve this. One is to make it look as though violence against women magically has no negative consequences. The content analysis of best-selling pornography by Bridges and colleagues found that 95 per cent of performers responded with either neutral or pleasurable expressions when aggressed against.[69] No need to feel concerned while masturbating to footage of a woman gagging on a man's penis if she actually likes throwing up, right?

Another nifty trick for quieting a consumer's conscience is to reassure him that while he is providing the demand for the footage produced – can you believe his luck? – it's actually supply driven. It's what *she* wants that's driving production. She's responsible. Phew. The website for porn series *Fuck a Fan* tempts consumers to enter their credit card details by boasting of one of the films: 'This tall winner gets to FUCK ALL THREE porn stars in their pussies and their hot mouths. This is certainly a great day for him and for our wonderful stars as well. Watch them each take turns pleasuring his average-sized cock and get his fingers and tongue up their cunts in the process.' Just in case would-be viewers have any qualms about how enthusiastic the women are about this, they are informed that its star happens to be 'a sexy big tit slut who loves nothing more than pleasing cock'. (The use of degrading terms to refer to women also helps dehumanise them as targets of aggression.)

Pornographers get a helping hand in their efforts to stop violence against women being a 'boner killer' from the pacifying effects of habituation. The way most porn is accessed also helps matters, with consumers able to relax in the knowledge of their anonymity when viewing it online. Added to which, the choreographed prostitution has taken place remotely, under someone else's direction, and consumed by countless others as well. All these factors help to dissolve any niggling feelings of responsibility in the viewer for what's being turned out by porn producers and turning up on his screen.

Pornographers harness conscience-crushing tactics to help their viewers enjoy footage of women being paid to endure sexual aggression. But this is not an industry propped up by phallic drones. Consumers courted by porn companies make a decision whether or not to reward pornographers' efforts to make sexual violence look harmless.

The sex trade is inevitable, the sex trade is inevitable, the sex trade is inevitable, the sex trade is inevitable. Convenient as this would be for some, and despite its repetition ad nauseam, it's a mythical claim with a very particular function. Whether the roots are placed in uncontainable carnal drives or otherworldly timelessness, it diverts attention from what drives the sex trade: the *entirely changeable* attitudes of those who constitute its demand.

When a buyer hands over money – whether it be in a strip club, on a porn site or in a brothel – he buys the 'privilege' of not having to consider whether the person stimulating his sexual arousal is attracted to him (or the person she's being paid to have sex with for him); whether or not she's 'in the mood'; what she likes sexually; whether it's uncomfortable, hurts or is degrading; what her boundaries are; what her insecurities might be; or how much pressure she's under to be there. He is getting instant access to a woman's body in a scenario where he, or the director, is in control. In short, he's paying for the power to use a woman as his sexual tool. One sex buyer described the pleasure of his purchase in an online review thus: 'Been waiting for a woman like her and [here] she is . . . Living fuck doll!'[70] Dehumanisation and misogyny enable the transaction. Without it, the sex trade could not survive.

MYTH 2: Being paid for sex is regular service work

Without saying a word, Sabine Constabel hands me a large tray of pastries and leads me to the exit of La Strada* – a cafe she set up nearly twenty years ago in Stuttgart. We step out into the heart of the city's red light district and walk about one hundred metres to a local brothel, which operates openly and legally. Thirteen years previously, in 2001, Germany's family minister and the Green Party's parliamentary floor leader had been photographed raising their champagne glasses in a toast with Felicitas Weigmann – a Berlin brothel owner.[1] The Bundestag had just legalised the prostitution trade, pimping and brothel-keeping included, and they were celebrating.[2]

We step into the narrow doorway of the brothel and make our way up the winding staircase. Four floors lead off it, each with a short corridor linking a series of small rooms – large enough to accommodate a single bed, a wardrobe, and not much else. The doors to some of the bedrooms are open, and Sabine approaches them to tell the young women inside that a doctor is visiting La Strada that evening so they can go for a check-up. As well as functioning as a cafe, La Strada also offers women involved in prostitution practical and psycho-

* The La Strada cafe run by Sabine Constabel is wholly distinct from the organisation La Strada International. To contact La Strada cafe visit www.inga-ev.de.

55

logical support services, and Sabine's work involves visiting local brothels to let women know about this. I hold out the cafe's pastries and most of the women take one, appreciatively saying 'Danke', although none speak German as a first language. Nearly all the women in this brothel are from Romania, Bulgaria and Hungary, as are most of the women in the Stuttgart prostitution trade. 'They cannot speak much German,' Sabine told me. 'They just have enough to convey the bare essentials one way or another. They learn the language here in the brothel or on the street.'

The youngest women in the brothel are eighteen; most aren't much older than twenty. As we talk with them, men make their way up and down the stairs, wandering along the corridors to see who is currently accepting 'custom'. 'They all live in the brothel,' Sabine says of the women here. 'They work, sleep and live in their one room in the brothel.' Not having a place of their own 'means that their leisure activities consist of perhaps going to La Strada, sometimes to the bakery or snack bar to have something to eat. When I fetch the women from the brothel by car to go to the doctor with them, for example, I have to return them practically to the front door because they have no geographical knowledge of their surroundings.' Each woman here has to pay the brothel owner €120 a day for the use of a room. That means she will usually have to perform sex acts on four men before she breaks even, more if she's paying off rent from previous days. I ask Sabine how long the women's doors are open to men walking the corridors. 'Seven days a week and about sixteen hours a day.'

The Prostitution Act passed by the Bundestag in 2001 legalised pimping and brothel-keeping,[3] thereby sanctioning them as legitimate forms of work (and, by extension, paying for sex as a legitimate consumer purchase). The law was sold to the parliament and public alike as a way to improve the 'working conditions' of women paid for sex. It was these conditions, not the prostitution itself, that were identified as the main source of any harm women experienced.[4] The government's solution was to allow brothels to issue employment contracts, so women had legal rights as employees. What transpired after the law was introduced has seen it dubbed the Pimp Protection Act.[5]

The bars and restaurants Sabine and I walked past that night had more regulations imposed on them than the brothel we were visiting. Unlike running a restaurant, opening up a brothel doesn't even require a permit. Any would-be brothel keeper can just open up shop and then register their new enterprise at the trade licensing office.[6] 'These days, even a convicted trafficker can do that perfectly legally,' Helmut Sporer, detective chief superintendent of the Crimes Squad in Augsburg, has pointed out.[7] Basic workplace health and safety rules don't even apply to most women in Germany's legal brothels. Why? Because for them to apply an individual has to be an employee.[8] And it is up to individual brothels whether or not they employ women or simply host them as 'independent contractors'. Overwhelmingly, they've opted for the latter. An evaluation of the Prostitution Act commissioned by Germany's Family Ministry found that 99 per cent of women in prostitution who were surveyed did not have an employment contract.[9] By 2013, just 44 people had officially registered their trade as prostitution in order to join the national insurance scheme.[10] The women Sabine and I met that night had to pay for the 'privilege' of being in the brothel; according to the state, they were simply one segment of Germany's self-employed workforce.

While the promised protections for women in the sex trade have not materialised, evidence of the benefits for brothel owners, flushed with their new government-approved status as legitimate business operators, has.[11] Stuttgart is now home to Paradise, one in a chain of so-called mega-brothels, and which cost over €6 million to build.[12] (Despite hosting thirty-one private rooms, Paradise is in fact dwarfed by Pascha, a twelve-storey brothel in Cologne.[13]) The Pussy Club was another brothel to open near Stuttgart.[14] For a flat rate of €70 during the day, €100 at night, the club promised men 'Sex with all women as long as you want, as often as you want and the way you want. Sex. Anal sex. Oral sex without a condom. Three-ways. Group sex. Gang bangs.'[15] During its opening weekend in 2009, police reported that around 1,700 men visited the brothel. According to *Der Spiegel* newspaper, after visiting the club that weekend, 'customers wrote in internet chat-rooms about the supposedly unsatisfactory service, complaining that the women were no longer as fit for use after a few hours'.[16] In 2004 the prostitution trade was estimated to be worth €6 billion. The figure is now thought to be more than double that.[17] With brothel-keeping now legitimate big business, a German television channel has been inspired to broadcast its own version of *Pimp My Ride*: *Pimp My Bordello*.[18]

Sitting in her office above the La Strada cafe, Sabine is unequivocal when I ask her who was the political driving force behind prostitution being legalised as a form of 'work'. 'It was people running the brothels . . . They wanted to earn money and they wanted these laws that made it possible to earn as much money as possible. Just like today.' Sabine set up the cafe so women in the local brothels could 'come to experience being here and receiving something without having to provide payment or a service in return'. As well as a meal, women can access wide-ranging support at La Strada, including healthcare and help finding employment. 'The aim of everything I do is exit [from prostitution], but in different ways,' Sabine says. Over nearly two decades, she has watched with horror at what this government-approved trade does to women who end up in Stuttgart's red light district. 'They are treated like dirt by the johns. The johns say to them, "You are a tart, you are a dirty whore, turn around, keep still, I'm going to fuck you now" – that's how they talk to them . . . The women endure many thousands of johns who are like that and they begin to believe this lousy nonsense.'

Sabine has also noticed a trend over recent years. The women arriving in the local brothels are getting younger. 'Because these young women provide a "good service", the kind of service the john wants, the demand for young women is very high. And now the industry has to provide eighteen-year-old girls.' One eighteen-year-old Sabine was supporting at the time I met her was Adrienn. Men began arriving at Adrienn's door in a brothel two weeks before her eighteenth birthday. She had been living in a children's home in Hungary until a family offered to take her in. It's a chain of events increasingly familiar to Sabine. 'The family says, "You have no job, you are a young girl, it's not easy for us to live, we have less money and there's a chance to go to Germany, earn money and that's for your family."' Adrienn was escorted to Stuttgart by a young man in the family. 'She came here when she was seventeen and was a virgin. She called her new father at home and begged him to let her stop the work. Her new father said no, she had to keep working.' Sabine has done what she can to help Adrienn. 'I told her everything I could. I made sure she knows everything, at least theoretically – whether she had really taken it in is less clear, where she can get help. She's got my phone number.' But so far Adrienn hasn't felt able to disobey the orders of her new 'family'.

I ask Sabine how Adrienn is coping. Her reply is hauntingly matter-of-fact. 'I think she has a small chance. It's likely that prostitution will simply destroy her . . . They have already given her drugs here because she couldn't work any more.' Sabine explained that young women like Adrienn are plied with drugs because 'for one thing they suffer pain, genuine physical pain . . . They are fucked from all sides.'

La Strada offers some rare respite to women and girls in the Stuttgart red light district, but year after year, women and girls keep arriving at the brothels – places the law now deems to be legitimate workplaces. 'They lose themselves,' says Sabine. 'I have women here, young women, very young women: they say, "I died here." I can empathise with what they mean. I believe them. I believe them that in reality the johns can damage the women to the extent that it is not possible for everything to go back to normal. In that way it is true. When they say, "I died", it's true. Part of them truly has been murdered by johns. It wasn't an accident. It was a crime.'

The notion that being paid to perform sex acts should be recognised as a kind of service work – 'sex work' – is the rationale underpinning legalised prostitution regimes. (And the implication, of course, is that paying someone for sex is recognised as a legitimate consumer activity.) It's an idea that has managed to unite an eclectic mix of left- and right-wing voices. Peter Frase, a member of the editorial board of *Jacobin*, a magazine billed as 'a leading voice of the American left',[19] is in favour of 'legalizing all forms of sex work for adults'.[20] He claims, 'Not only does sex work destabilize the work ideology, it also conflicts with a bourgeois ideal of private, monogamous sexuality.'[21] Tim Worstall, writing for British right-wing think-tank, the Adam Smith Institute, shares Frase's policy conclusion, though his reasoning contrasts somewhat. As a type of commercial activity, Worstall insists the prostitution trade is 'obviously free market'[22] and, providing force isn't involved, 'renting out body parts is and should be no different from lending them out for fun or for free'.[23] The framing of prostitution as 'sex work' is by no means confined to the political edges. The terminology, and its underlying logic, has been employed by a host of intergovernmental institutions, including the World Health Organization (WHO), United Nations Population Fund (UNFPA) and the Joint United Nations Programme on HIV/AIDS (UNAIDS) in their reports and recommendations on the trade.[24] The drive to recognise the global phenomenon of men paying (predominantly) women for sex as a regular consumer transaction has also benefited from the advocacy (and financial backing) of billionaire financier George Soros's Open Society Foundations. The organisation pushes for the language of labour to be used in relation to prostitution because, they say, 'the terms "sex work" and "sex worker" recognize that sex work is work'.[25]

Right. So if 'sex work is work', then presumably if an airline company requires all its female flight attendants to offer male passengers blow-jobs, as well as drinks and snacks, that's all right?* What about City firms stipulating that female employees must have sex with male clients as part of their corporate entertaining duties? OK? How about when a male boss asks his female secretary to give him a blow-job? It's the kind of scenario feminists have spent decades working to get recognised as sexual harassment. But, I guess, if this is ordinary work then at worst the requested task is merely outside her job description?

---

* In 2008, Michael O'Leary, CEO of low-cost airline Ryanair, did actually 'joke' at a press conference that business class in their new long-haul fleet would offer 'beds and blow-jobs'. Economy passengers would have to pay for any luxuries but 'in business class it will all be free – including the blow-jobs'.[26]

In some countries, specialist exiting services are provided for women wanting to get out of the sex trade, offering targeted and sustained support such as counselling. But if it's just regular service work, why would exiting services be necessary?

No doubt sex buyers will be delighted to learn that, if prostitution really is a form of service work, they become service users. Service users with *rights*. I asked Philip Kolvin QC and Clare Parry, barristers at Cornerstone Barristers in London, what the legal consequences would be if prostitution was actually enshrined as work in UK law. They told me that as it would constitute the provision of a service, the relevant law it would be governed by requires that the service

> be supplied with reasonable care and skill. In the event of a breach, the payer may be relieved of the obligation to pay, and may also sue for damages including loss of enjoyment, going beyond the price of the service itself. It is hard to see on what basis a court could refuse to entertain litigation on the topic. The case might be that the customer did not obtain relief or the prostitute did not perform satisfactorily.

In the last chapter, I highlighted how sex buyers demand that the women they pay provide them with a 'good service'. If prostitution were 'sex work' in law, they would be legally entitled to this. Another way a sex buyer could exercise his legal entitlements: 'There would be likely to be an implied term that the prostitute was free of STDs, so that if a client was infected, that might also give rise to a claim for damages.'

It's not only sex buyers who acquire legal powers over women in prostitution when 'sex work' is translated from a slogan to the statute books. If he pays her, she has to pay the state. As a regular 'worker', a person in prostitution would be obliged to pay tax. Fail to do so, Kolvin and Parry point out, and she could be 'pursued in the normal ways by the tax authorities, including bankruptcy, seizing possessions, and getting orders in magistrates and county court'. If a woman in the prostitution trade is officially a self-employed contractor she has no employment rights whatsoever. But if a brothel or escort business does employ her, theoretically 'she could be dismissed for gross misconduct for refusal to have sex with a particular person or for not turning up for work'. So, if the law really did accept the claim that prostitution is just regular service work – 'sex work' – a woman could quite legally be fired from her job for saying no to sex.

And yet, Germany's prostitution law does not entirely accept this. Despite legalising brothel-keeping and pimping, they have (thankfully) failed to pursue the 'sex work' sloganeering to all of its logical conclusions, belying claims that the activity concerned is a regular consumer transaction. While they do tax women paid for sex, officially it's up to her whether she does or doesn't 'service a customer' on any particular occasion.[27] (Although, as I'll show in a later chapter, enforcing this kind of provision is a different matter.) Her legal relationship with a sex buyer, as well as her legal relationship with a brothel if they directly employ her, is designated as 'a contract with unilateral obligations'.[28]

There's a reason states can't follow the sloganeering through and treat being paid for sex as 'a job like any other': because prostitution isn't 'sex work'. It's sexual abuse.

The chilling absurdity of claiming that what's taking place on porn sets and in brothels can be suitably framed as an innocuous consumer transaction is put into sharp focus with a cursory glance at a UK government website, This Is Abuse, which offers young people basic guidance on sexual consent:

> More things to look out for to make sure you have consent:

- When it comes to sex or physical closeness you should feel safe with your partner, be able to trust them and feel that they would respect you whatever your decision.

- Good communication between you both will help to ensure you know how your partner feels about sex or physical closeness. It is a good idea to check things out with your partner by asking if they are enjoying what you are doing and asking if they want to continue.

- Reading body language is also important. If your partner is relaxed it is likely that they feel comfortable. If they are tense, they may be nervous or frightened and are probably trying to hide how they really feel.

- Someone doesn't have to say the word 'NO' to withhold their permission, there are lots of ways they might say they don't want to do something or have sex.

- Look out for signs of someone not consenting to sex – sometimes people might find it hard to say anything at all if they don't want to have sex, so for example if someone stops kissing you or doesn't want to be hugged or held, this could be a sign of non-consent. Don't ignore it.

- *If one person doesn't want to have sex, the other person just needs to accept that, it's not OK to try and change their minds as pressuring someone into sex is rape and there are consequences.*[29] (Italics mine)

The whole *point* of the sex industry is that it offers men the chance to buy sexual access to women who do not want to have sex with them. That is the whole point. Otherwise they *wouldn't have to pay.*

Masking its fundamental purpose thus becomes the primary PR challenge for the prostitution, pornography and strip club trades if they are to survive – maybe even thrive – in a society that has decided, at least in principle, that women are not subordinate fuck objects and rape is a bad thing.

Perhaps the single most effective strategy they've hit upon so far is to pump out the myth contained in the term 'sex work': the myth that it is possible to commodify consent. That sexual consent is a 'thing' that can be bought and sold and we can all still talk with a straight face about there being such concepts as healthy sexual relationships and meaningful consent. But if while having sex with someone you feel repulsed by them touching you, afraid of what they might do, degraded and humiliated by the sexual acts, hurt by the hateful words they're whispering in your ear, sore because he's the fifth man you've had sex with today, exhausted from it all, traumatised, *abused* – the fact that you'll get a bit of cash at the end does not change this fact. There is no invisible hand in the prostitution market that magically disappears the lived experience of sexual abuse.

On the contrary. The very act of paying someone to participate in sex acts is abusive. It is persuasion. It is pressure. It is 'have sex with me, continue having sex with me, make sure that I'm satisfied, or there will be financial consequences for you'. It is 'get down on your knees and give me a blow-job and I'll see that you get that cocaine fix you're craving'. It's 'take off your clothes and let me and my mate take it in turns and we'll agree to help you pay this month's rent'. The special promise of strip clubs, porn sites and brothels, however, is that they unburden customers of the hassle of finding women with the necessary pressures and life experiences to lead them to this scenario. The bidding is taken care of. The women and girls are assembled. All he has to do is hand over money.

There's a condition, though. The unwritten contract the standard 'consumer' enters into with the sex trade requires that not only will most of the coercive leg-work involved in providing a ready selection of women be taken care of, he won't have to hear about it. A 'good service' requires a smile and some reassurance: 'I love it. Harder. I was born for this.' What Sabine described to me as 'the show'.

But what if sex trade users weren't obliged with this script? What if they had to listen to how the women in front of them, under them, really felt? What if they heard about the chain of events that brought each woman to the strip club, the porn set, the brothel? *What do the 'consumers' invest in not knowing?*

Before

Trouble at home, and trouble with money, were what prompted Jessie to answer the job advert that resulted in footage of her having sex for money being watched around the world. (Bear in mind, though, that Jessie only found out the job was porn, not 'modelling', once she was actually sitting in the office of the agency that placed the ad.) 'I had just got out of high school,' Jessie explained to me over Skype from her home in the US. 'I was living with my sister at the time and her husband, which she's not with any more because he was a douchebag. He brainwashed her into kicking me out when I was eighteen and I had nowhere to go. And I was just like, "How am I going to make money?"' Other factors that kept Jessie in her seat, rather than bolting for the agent's door, were less immediately pressing. She said, despite feeling 'uncomfortable' at the prospect of doing pornography,

There was something inside me that kind of felt like I
had to do that, that I wouldn't be successful at anything
else. Because, like, when I was a teenager I watched a
lot of, I don't know if you're aware of the Playboy Show?
Not the actual porn shows – it was a reality show. But it
was like with these Playboy models . . . I always had this
illusion that for a girl in this society to become successful
or wealthy or something like that she has to show off her
body. So, that's kind of how my mentality was at that
time.

Being repeatedly sexually assaulted as a child, the first time
when she was ten, was pivotal to Tanja Rahm's entry into the
Danish prostitution trade. 'It was like my sexuality didn't be-
long to me. It was something men could take if they wanted
it,' she told me. By the time Tanja was twenty, the idea of
picking up the phone and calling a brothel felt like a logical
act: 'Then I would at least get some money for the things men
did to me . . . It was like my vagina was a separate part from
me which I didn't think of as something pleasurable, but more
like a thing men wanted from me and which I had to give
them to feel that I was worth something.' There were no alarm
bells ringing for Tanja in the beginning. The men's behaviour
just felt normal. 'They often tried to do something they knew
they wasn't allowed to, like putting fingers inside my vagina,
kiss me, pull the condom off to come all over me and things
like that. But I was used to getting my boundaries violated
from my childhood, so I didn't really think anything of it.'

There was nothing that felt normal the night Lucy began her first shift in a London lap-dancing club. The industry's shop-front bore scant relation to what she found inside. 'I had a view that they were glamorous and that I would make lots of money going there, working there, and it would be exciting,' she told me, curled up on her sofa as we sat in her London flat. The job ad she had spotted in a performing arts newspaper called for 'table dancers'. 'I didn't even know what table dancing was. I thought table dancing was dancing on tables and I didn't quite know how that would work or why you would dance on a table but that was in my mind.' Walking into the club that first night quickly cleared things up. 'In reality table dancing means lap dancing and lap dancing means being naked and rubbing yourself on men . . . There's no dancing. Not really. It's not really dancing.'

But while it never felt routine, like Tanja, Lucy described how having her personal boundaries bulldozed helped clear a path to the sex trade. During her late teens, Lucy was raped by a man she met on a night out. 'That is the spiral,' she said. 'On one hand, you've had your power taken away and that was through a sexual act and then you feel powerless and uncomfortable in the world . . . And then there's this other belief I suppose, which I think we have particularly as young women, which is that your primary source of power is your sexual power.' The rape left Lucy feeling as though she couldn't 'be a sexual person or express my sexuality because look at what happens when you do. Like, look at what can happen when you do. But here's this place that I could do that and there's bouncers and security guards.' But that craved promise of power turned out to be a particularly cruel industry myth. 'That is not how you go about empowering yourself if what you want is sexual empowerment,' Lucy said, her tone now incredulous. 'It's ludicrous to imagine. And the only way that you could imagine it is if you don't really know what goes on inside, if you don't really understand what it is, or if you're still invested in it.'

Childhood marks the point of entry for a significant portion of women involved in the sex trade. A report by the UK government noted that a staggering 50 per cent of women in prostitution are estimated to have become involved before the age of eighteen.[30] Research carried out with people in prostitution in nine countries across five continents found pretty much the same: 47 per cent had become involved as children.[31] Childhood sexual abuse also turns up with disturbing regularity in the histories of those who enter the sex trade. Interviews conducted with 100 women involved in prostitution in Canada uncovered that 82 per cent had been sexually abused as children.[32] Similarly, a survey of 71 women engaged in a prostitution exiting scheme in the US found almost 80 per cent of the women had experienced childhood sexual abuse.[33] It was also flagged up as a pivotal factor by Julian Heng when I spoke to him about his work over the past nine years with men involved in prostitution. While it is overwhelmingly women and girls who are paid for sex, in 2006 Julian set up Open Road, an NHS service in Glasgow specifically for men who sold sex, because it had become apparent that there were men in the city centre 'using sex for payment on-street as a means of survival behaviour. Not in any way related to sexual identity or sexual preference but purely as a means of survival, because they were rough sleeping, they were destitute.' A recurring theme in these men's accounts of their journeys to prostitution was a combination of 'adverse effects in childhood, homelessness at an early age and then the association with the drug using peer group'.

A few years after Open Road started, it was clear that one childhood factor in particular stood out among the group of men Julian was working with: 'Their disclosure of childhood sexual abuse was way above 50 per cent.' Such early experiences of enduring abuse could play a critical role, Julian suggested, in the men being able to 'rationalise and accommodate the experience of unwanted sex [of prostitution] as something they might actually be able to adapt to and cope with'. Also consistent with women's experiences of prostitution, it was solely men who were paying them for sex. Like the phenomenon of men paying women for sex, Julian describes men paying men for sex as 'a form and an expression of gender-based violence', fuelled by 'that male privilege and dominance that comes from gender inequality in society'.

Racism, financial hardship and marginalisation also litter people's pathways into the sex trade. A New Zealand study published in 2001 found that despite constituting just 7 per cent of the female population between the ages of fifteen and forty-four in Christchurch, women with Maori ancestry made up 19 per cent of those identified in the local prostitution trade.[34] Research in Canada suggests First Nations women are overrepresented in the prostitution trade.[35] 'Aboriginal women are especially vulnerable to prostitution and [it's] a human rights violation,' says Bridget Perrier, who co-founded the Canadian group Sextrade101 with fellow activist Natasha Falle. The organisation provides support services for people exploited through prostitution, as well as public education about the reality of the sex trade. Bridget herself was just twelve years old when she was first sexually exploited. 'I didn't choose prostitution. Prostitution chose me. Due to colonialism, due to me being sexually abused, me being given up for adoption.' In the UK, research has revealed that up to one third of young women involved in street prostitution have previously spent time in local authority care.[36] I was discussing this one day with a colleague of mine who oversees a prostitution exiting scheme in London, providing accommodation and vital specialist support for sixteen women at any one time who want to leave prostitution. She mentioned in passing that at one point, all of the women in this residential programme had previously been through the same local authority care system.

Poverty can of course play a highly influential role in women's entry into prostitution. However, bluntly asserting that poverty is the singular cause of the prostitution trade fails to acknowledge that men's poverty has not begot a global demand from women to pay them for sex acts, that without men's demand there would be no trade at all, or the highly specific abuses that so commonly characterise women's entry.

Sex inequality cracks open the prostitution trade, while particular vulnerabilities push some women closer to the edge. 'What all of them have in common is what happened to them before prostitution became an alternative,' social worker Miki Nagata told me when I visited her office at the Prostitution Unit in Stockholm. The unit provides support for people currently involved in prostitution as well as those wanting to exit; support like counselling, help with housing and access to training. 'It doesn't matter if you come from a very rich home in Stockholm or come from a poor family,' Miki says, 'because what we can see with all people we meet here – they have some kind of neglect and abuse in their background and that's why prostitution became an alternative . . . We never see any kind of free choice, but different kinds of coercion.'

So when Miki and her colleagues ask people who visit the Unit about their reasons for being in prostitution, the recurring answers include, 'to get confirmation or validation, or "This is all I know how to do, this is all I'm worth" . . . I have clients who say, "I've been doing this [being sexually abused] all my life, now I can get money for it at least."' The reasons are never 'only about money'. It's a common misconception, Miki says. 'I have never ever met anyone who says this is my job, this is a great job. That's why we never use words like "sex work" or "sex workers". We don't even use the word "prostitute" – because this is something you do, it's not something you are. You have an experience of prostitution but you are a human being and have many other experiences in your life.'

Indeed, far from solving financial problems, an analysis by economics professor Linda DeRiviere, published in the journal *Feminist Economics*, found that prostitution had a permanent detrimental impact on women's lifetime earnings. A significant portion of the money women in the study earned from performing sex acts on men was siphoned off, for instance, through payments to pimps, escort agency owners and drugs to cope with the prostitution. 'Net annual surplus funds after subtracting the substantial costs associated with sex-trade activities are less than 8 per cent of gross earnings,'[37] DeRiviere reported. Ultimately, being in the sex trade significantly reduced women's lifelong earnings, in large part because of the serious physical and mental health problems it left them with.

For Mia de Faoite, it was heroin that chaperoned her to the Burlington Road in Dublin; a place she knew would provide a steady stream of men with their eyes shut to her addiction, but their wallets and car doors open. 'I went out, I suppose you could say, with encouragement from my ex,' she told me. 'To me it was a shock obviously because I was thinking, "God, I haven't been with a man in eleven years" or whatever it was. [My girlfriend] was saying, "It's not really about that. You just, you know." Anyway she was right on that. You do just kind of disconnect.' Mia was thirty-three at the time and thought she would be able to handle it for a few months. 'But I had no idea of the world I was about to step into and it got hold of me fairly quick.' Three nights a week, for the next six years, Mia would stand and wait on the Burlington Road.

The very first night she walked out onto that street is etched on her memory.

> That first person pulled up and took me to a big car park . . . The first thing I ever did in prostitution was sex[ual intercourse]. . . . I didn't know that I could say, 'Oh I don't do that.' I didn't know what to do. I was high. And high and frightened is kind of a weird state. So I did it and I just felt like I'd crossed the line.

'Something broke,' Mia says. 'Something personal inside broke.'

During

Regardless of routes in, the fact that the sex trade is founded upon the absence of mutual sexual desire means the principle predicament becomes how to endure repeated sexual abuse. Not just endure it, but appear to want it – lest it be deemed a 'bad service'.

There is one endurance strategy above all others that women I interviewed mentioned using, and which reappears again and again in the research: dissociation. Rape Crisis Scotland describe dissociation as 'when the brain "disconnects" from what is happening. It goes somewhere "safe". Other words for this include "switching off" or "spacing out".'[38] Dissociation, they explain, is 'a natural response to the trauma of sexual violence'.

'It's no coincidence that everyone seems to know to do this,' Diane Martin CBE told me. It's something Diane has both seen and felt, having been involved in what she calls 'the supposed "high end" of prostitution' in her late teens, and subsequently spending nearly two decades supporting women exploited through the trade. 'You need to find a way to cope by mentally switching off from what you are experiencing in the moment. The narrative in your head is worlds apart from the fantasy the man has constructed for his own benefit. I'm a qualified counsellor but I knew what "dissociation" and "splitting" was before I ever read about them in a book.' Rachel Moran, who became involved in the prostitution trade in Ireland at the age of fifteen after becoming homeless, says dissociation is 'as necessary to the prostituted woman as typing is to the secretary . . . It is the most necessary tool in the very limited arsenal you use to protect yourself.'

Sitting in her Stuttgart office above La Strada cafe, as women downstairs had their dinner before heading back to the brothels, Sabine Constabel described to me what can happen if women and girls don't get sufficiently close to this metaphysical feat. 'I've seen many, many, many women who became psychotic because they can't dissociate. They don't have a strategy. So they become psychotic. Or they become so addicted to drugs that they can no longer be exploited by the sex industry.'

Strangely enough, it turns out that legalising brothels and dubbing what goes on inside as 'sex work' does not magically transform women into insentient sex dolls. 'They experience it as rape,' Sabine says.

> They say no to the sex, not to the money . . . They get close to this man, they allow themselves to be grabbed, they let themselves be touched, they move their bodies towards him, and simultaneously everything inside them retreats . . . That's why they cannot stay in contact with the act. They can't stay there while the john is screwing them. They have to get themselves to safety somehow . . . And that's the crazy thing about prostitution. It causes enormous amounts of psychological stress.

For some, that stress reaches intolerable levels. 'They shatter,' she says.

On her very first day shooting porn, Jessie witnessed one particular technique that's sometimes used to construct a makeshift psychological refuge.

> One of the female performers actually had her bong with her on set . . . She was like, 'Oh, do you want some?' I was like, 'Is this OK?' Like, you know, I was so naive I thought that you had to be professional like a regular job so I wanted to be completely sober and she was like, 'Oh, no, it's fine' . . . And then there was another girl that I saw that she looked off. So I was like, 'Are you OK? Are you high or something?' And she just started giggling. She was like, 'Well, I took a pill.' I'm like, 'What?' She was like,

'Yeah, well, yeah I'm rolling now.' I was like, 'What is that?' She was like 'Oh, I'm on ecstasy.' . . . I learned very quickly that those girls need something to get through the scenes.

But it was only when she found herself using this endurance strategy that what was happening really sank in. 'I started drinking more. Kind of, you know, disassociating myself. Just like those girls that I met on my first scene did. And then that was when it kind of hit me. "Oh, OK. That's why these girls have to take pills or have to be high."'

Professor Linda DeRiviere's research with women into the lifetime costs of prostitution found that over two-thirds of women interviewed either did not use alcohol or drugs, or weren't addicted to them, before their involvement in prostitution. And only 12.9 per cent of women reported that paying for drugs and alcohol was their sole motivation for entering the trade. Yet once in prostitution, 95 per cent of the women developed a serious addiction. This was consistent, the research concluded, with drugs being used as a 'coping mechanism'.[39] Women were self-medicating in order to endure prostitution.

Initially, Tanja Rahm didn't think she would need drugs to get through prostitution. 'I was used to getting my boundaries violated from my childhood.' For the first couple of months in the brothel, she says, things seemed to be going OK. 'I thought I was in so much control. Finally, I was the one saying yes or no, I was the one deciding what the men could buy from me.' But proof that she remained inescapably anchored to the abuse being enacted on her body soon began to show. 'I suddenly found myself showering for hours. I was trying to wash it all off me, sometimes with a hard sponge. But even if I did so, I could still smell the men, the brothel, and the semen. It was like it was all inside of me. So I began to get up from bed in the middle of the night just to take a shower, sitting under the water for hours.' Attempting to dissociate during prostitution took a heavy toll. 'To shut down the depressive feelings while you had to pretend that you liked what the buyers did to you almost made me crazy.'

Tanja turned to cocaine for help accomplishing the feat of being simultaneously present and absent in the brothel. But it was ultimately an impossible challenge. 'I hated the money and I hated what was going on. I just couldn't pretend that I liked it any more. I couldn't pretend when I was with the men and I couldn't lie to myself any more. The men got rude because my body was there but "I" wasn't.'

As a tactic for enduring acute trauma, dissociation can open up an ephemeral escape hatch.

But it can work too well. As researchers at the universities of Calgary, Saskatchewan and Manitoba noted in a joint study of women's experiences in prostitution, 'trauma reactions also keep young women involved in prostitution by leading them to ignore or suppress their own emotional distress . . . Self-destructive, self-injurious behaviours and suicidal ideation are common trauma reactions.'[40] Dissociation can deactivate vital internal alarm systems.

Ultimately, mentally 'splitting off' isn't an impenetrable shield against the psychological blows inflicted through repeated sexual abuse. A study of people involved in prostitution in nine countries found that 68 per cent met the diagnostic criteria for post-traumatic stress disorder (PTSD) – comparable to the rate detected among survivors of state-sponsored torture.[41]

'Why don't they just leave?'

Crystal, who exited prostitution in the UK over five years ago, still has PTSD. I asked her what it was like living day to day during her time in the prostitution trade.

> You feel dirty all the time . . . You have men's come on or in your body, their sweat on you, aches and pains from the sex acts and the memory of their pawing touch all over your body. You get sore. There is no respite – if someone bangs your cervix, if you tear, if you bruise, there's no time to heal . . . Even when you've showered you feel dirty.

Crystal regularly found herself waking up in the middle of the night 'with palpitations and sweats, mental with PTSD and addiction, and [I would] tell myself, "Never again. I can't do that again." And I'd think about the men touching me, man after man, most of them faceless in my remembrance, and I'd get sick. Very rarely I'd cry,' she says. 'Sometimes all the control you have is guarding your reactions.'

Crystal first became involved in prostitution through an abusive boyfriend, who pimped her to fund his drug habit.

> The slide into it all was gradual, painful and confusing . . . The violence got worse, and what he wanted me to do and made me do sexually got worse . . . At the time, I felt like I was disintegrating. I was vulnerable when I got with my ex, I was just losing my mum to cancer, which I think left me particularly open to being used. And it didn't feel like there were any choices.

This phenomenon of women being pimped by a 'boyfriend' figure highlights one of many connections and parallels between prostitution and domestic violence. A trafficker jailed in Mexico in 2009 described to the *Guardian* how feigning the role of boyfriend was a tactic he used to entrap women in the trade. On his first ever job as a 'recruiter' he approached a young woman who was a domestic worker at the time. 'Once I got her laughing, I knew I was in with a chance . . . Then I got the sun, the moon and the stars down from the sky for her.'[42] Within a month this young woman, whom the trafficker had feigned wanting to marry, was paying off a debt he had fabricated by prostituting on the streets. 'I never had any problem activating my girls,' he said. 'It was really easy for me.'

I discussed the kind of abusive tactics used by this trafficker, and experienced by Crystal, with Polly Neate, chief executive of UK national domestic violence charity, Women's

Aid. When it comes to discussions about women in abusive relationships, she said, 'The thing I get asked more than anything else is "why don't they just leave?" The fundamental thing to understand in answering that question is coercive control, and the power that a perpetrator can exert over a victim. And I think that applies to all kinds of ways in which women are dominated and abused by men; domestic violence is one of those, prostitution is another.' Where coercive control is being used,

> Very commonly it will take quite some time for her
> to realise that she's being abused. And some of that is
> because just like with a boyfriend-pimp relationship, a
> lot of that presents initially as what we as a society see as
> very romantic behaviour; excessive jealousy, rewarding
> subservient behaviours with presents . . . So it can take
> quite a long time. And a perpetrator will build on that
> and gradually increase control of the victim. And it can
> take quite some time to break out of that and actually
> recognise that you are being abused.

There is a common misconception that to recognise prostitution as violence, and the actions of pimps and men who pay for sex as abusive, is to somehow deny the agency of the woman concerned. It isn't. We know that people make decisions and take steps to manage situations in which someone is perpetrating harm against them. That's not in question. Yet regardless of how a person responds at any particular time, which will be influenced by a multitude of factors, it in no way shape or form excuses the abusive actions of the perpetrator. 'I just think that's a really important thing to understand about women in any sort of abusive situation is that their own coping strategies inevitably then reinforce their own perception of the situation. So not only the way outsiders blame them for being there, but the way in which they end up blaming themselves for being there.' When it comes to how sex inequality and sexist violence impacts on women's daily lives, Polly rightly points out that 'we have to respect how individual women deal with the situation that we are all in. But we also have to be really fearless in identifying, together, what that situation is and what needs to change about it.'

Crystal has dug about as deep as it's possible to go to build a new life following years of what can only be described as sexual torture. She has a child. She has a home. She blogs about her experiences and meets with politicians to lobby for the kind of exiting services that weren't available to her (the acute practical and psychological barriers to leaving prostitution being yet another parallel with domestic violence situations). And yet, the trauma follows her like a shadow.

I still feel like I lost a part of myself back there – and there's no getting her back. I still have PTSD. I still split and have different heads. I still freeze up sometimes and become mute. I get nightmares and flashbacks and intrusive thoughts. At times I feel completely overwhelmed by it and completely lost. At these times, the thought returns to me that any idea of trying to live a normal life is impossible. I feel cut off, like I don't fit in. How can I in a society that says that what I went through is just ordinary work, is liberating and empowering, is a choice and to be respected? I feel sold out at every level. I save to pay for therapy because that's important and I have to believe that that will help. I have done so much to distance myself from where I was – to have some dignity, to live an ordinary life, to build a relationship and be open to being loved and loving. But sometimes it feels incredibly fragile and I feel like I'm falling off the edge of the world and there's no one to catch me.

Layers of violence

Compounding the sexual abuse and objectification which is at the core of prostitution is layer upon layer of additional violence. A US study of mortality rates found that women involved in prostitution are nearly 18 times more likely to be murdered than women not in the trade.[43] Of the analysed murder cases of women with involvement in prostitution, over a third of the women were killed while soliciting. The researchers noted that 'clients perpetrate a large proportion of the lethal and nonlethal violence' and that 'no population of women studied previously has had a crude mortality rate, standardized mortality ratio, or percentage of deaths due to murder even approximating those observed in our cohort'. Research has also uncovered that over 50 per cent of women in street prostitution in the UK have been raped or sexually assaulted, the vast majority of these attacks committed by sex buyers.[44]

For most of the six years Mia de Faoite spent in prostitution in Ireland, she stuck to the streets. 'I stood beside a garden and in the summer the water feature used to go on so I used to like sitting there.' Outdoors also felt safer to Mia. 'One main reason: you can run.' The sex acts would take place in cars or secluded spots near the road. One night, however, Mia and her friend Jenny agreed to prostitution indoors at a Christmas party. They were both gang raped. 'I thought I was going to lose my mind. I actually thought my mind was going to explode. I think the only thing that stopped it from doing it was the young girl that was with me that night was younger and I felt I had to mind her.' After the rapes, Mia's heroin use escalated, in order to 'remain numb'. But the need to fund that coping mechanism pushed her back out on to the streets. 'It's just this circle.' Jenny's addiction also spiralled. But she didn't survive. Jenny died of a drugs overdose two months after the gang rape. 'To many her death would just be another sad statistic,' Mia later wrote, 'but to me her life will always be of value.'

Research in three UK cities found that half of women in outdoor prostitution, and a quarter of women in indoor prostitution, reported having been subject to violence by a sex buyer in the previous six months.[45] Of the violence they had ever experienced at the hands of sex buyers, women on the streets most frequently reported being kicked, slapped or punched, while women in saunas or flats most frequently reported attempted rape (17 per cent of women based indoors had experienced this, as had 28 per cent of women on the streets). A separate study involving over one hundred women engaged in flat-based prostitution in London highlighted how an indoor setting can have its own particular coercive influence.[46] Each day women had to pay up to £250 in rent, as well as up to £60 a day for a 'maid' (who in practice often operated like a pimp, sometimes controlling which sex buyers the women saw), plus a range of other expenses. 'You've got to get through, like, ten punters before you've made your rent and maid. And after that you might not do any more, so you don't make any money,' one woman reported. On average, a woman was paid for sex by 76 men each week. Per day, 'many' women were paid to have sex with between 20 and 30 men. The study revealed the role so-called maids could play in protecting women from violence by sex buyers was 'minimal'. During the sex acts, the women are of course alone with the men, and a common incident reported by women was a sex buyer becoming violent if she refused his extra demands during sex, or if she agreed but only on condition he paid extra. 'What links or cuts across women's own accounts, regardless of the setting, is the potential for client violence,' concluded the researchers.

Outside

The Economist's 2014 editorial warding off 'puritans' and 'do-gooders' from meddling with the sex trade insists that governments should 'leave consenting adults who wish to buy and sell sex to do so safely and privately online.'[47] This builds on the claim that prostitution is 'sex work' by attempting to frame that 'work' as simply a series of individual, private exchanges, set apart from the rest of society. Milton Friedman, the late economist and proponent of unbridled free-market capitalism, inferred much the same when asked about prostitution in 2006. 'You put a willing buyer [with] a willing seller, and it's up to them. You can argue with them that it's foolish, you can argue with them that it's a bad thing to do, but I don't see any justification for bringing the police into it.'[48] But the sex industry, like any market, doesn't operate in a vacuum, leaving the rest of society miraculously untouched by its presence. Markets are, as philosopher Debra Satz says, 'social institutions': '*all* markets depend for their operation on background property rules and a complex of social, cultural, and legal institutions.'[49] Markets are a matter for everyone. Brothels, porn sets and strip clubs produce what in the 'sex work' discourse would aptly be described as externalities – costs imposed by market exchanges on parties not directly involved. The suggestion that the sex trade affects no one outside of the lap-dancing club, the porn set, the brothel, is pure fantasy. The myths pumped out by the trade to neutralise potential opposition and crack open new market opportunities affect us all – precisely the kind of myths identified in this book: that sexual consent can be purchased and not have its very essence destroyed in the process; that men need and are entitled to (paid) sex and will resort to rape if denied it; that the sexual objectification of women is harmless; and so on.

Nor are the 'externalities' spewed out by the sex trade confined to the present. They affect women and girls not yet caught up in the industry. The current acceptance and legitimisation of prostitution, pornography and stripping as 'sex work' increases the future likelihood of women and girls being sexually exploited. Informally adopting and then ordering the seventeen-year-old Adrienn to a Stuttgart brothel was a viable and attractive option for her 'family' in Hungary precisely because there was an existing legal and lucrative prostitution trade in Germany, with a ready supply of punters willing to hand over cash that she could send back. (How it actually panned out is that Adrienn handed over the money to the young male family member who accompanied her on the cross-border trip. It's he who supplies the drugs enabling the now traumatised Adrienn to continue 'working'.)

Trades weave themselves into the fabric of society. We know this. We place all kinds of restrictions and prohibitions on markets precisely because of this. Because the risks, particularly to the most vulnerable and marginalised in society, are just too high. Sales of human organs, voting rights, bonded labour contracts; commercial exchanges that people may agree to participate in without a gun being held to their head are nonetheless deemed legally off-limits. It's the line in the sand societies draw to say that the harm to those directly involved, to third parties, or to the bedrock principles necessary for equal citizenship, is simply too great. Some trades are too toxic to tolerate.

A basic principle that is utterly indispensable to ending violence against women, not to mention to our fundamental concept of humanity, is that sexual abuse is *never* acceptable. Not even when the perpetrator has some spare cash and the person he's abusing needs money. Cheerleaders of brothels, porn sets and strip clubs would have us believe that the sex trade levitates above the level of social values and cultural beliefs. But no one can opt out of its effects. A market in sexual exploitation, accepted and tolerated, influences who we all are as individuals, and who we are as a people.

Looking in

The steady creep of 'sex work' into twenty-first century vernacular is neither incidental nor accidental. The term didn't just pop up and go viral. The Global Network of Sex Work Projects (NSWP), an organisation that openly campaigns for brothel-keeping and pimping to be recognised as legitimate jobs, credits itself as 'largely responsible' for 'sex work' replacing prostitution as the go-to terminology for institutions like UNAIDS and WHO.[50] 'More than mere political correctness,' NSWP proudly state, 'this shift in language had the important effect of moving global understandings of sex work toward a labour framework.'[51]

The fact that prostitution involves sexual acts and some kind of payment is, of course, a given. But engaging with it first and foremost as a labour issue, using the term 'sex work' as if it was an adequate and appropriate shorthand for what takes place in strip clubs, porn sets and brothels, serves a deeply political goal. Not only does this framework shrink the field of analysis to the 'seller' (to the exclusion of men's demand and its social impact); crucially, it hides what should be front and centre of our response to the transaction: the inherent sexual abuse.

A perennial feature of political struggles are battles over how issues are framed. It's the all-important tussle for the terms of debate. Frames matter because, as researchers at Ohio State and Purdue universities found, they 'influence opinions by stressing specific values, facts, and other considerations, endowing them with greater apparent relevance to the issue than they might appear to have under an alternative frame.'[52] The 'labour framework' NSWP congratulates itself on promulgating is powerful because of what it manages to cut out of the picture.

'All that does is make it seem OK,' Crystal tells me when I ask what she thinks about her experiences in brothels being labelled as 'sex work'.

> It minimises the harm . . . you're naked, being touched intimately by a stranger, being fucked by a stranger, having them whisper sick things in your ear about your body and how dirty you are and how you like what they're doing – as if! I tried to dissociate but that is only ever partially possible . . . It is the ultimate invasion: they are in your head and they are inside your body.

The 'sex work' frame demands that people think and speak about the practice of men paying women to have sex with them as if it were a mundane consumer transaction. It demands the denial of the misogyny, objectification and sexual violence at its very core, and functions as a kind of linguistic crowd control: 'You're not anti-sex, are you? People need to work, right? Well, then, hurry along.'

I asked Sarah Veale, then the head of equality and employment rights at Britain's Trades Union Congress (TUC), whether she thought it appropriate to apply a 'labour framework' to the sex trade. 'In a civilised society sexual exploitation cannot be counted as a labour market activity; prostitution is sexual exploitation,' she said. Unions can best support women who are being sexually exploited, Sarah suggested, by 'helping them to find real work, with dignity, fair treatment, mutuality and safety'.

As a decoy strategy, positioning the sex trade first and foremost as a labour issue is substantially more effective than wheeling out the 'empowerment frame', which asks people to believe that the sex trade is a full-on shot in the arm for feminism. (Like Hugh Hefner arguing that '*Playboy* and the Playboy clubs were the end of sexism.'[53]) 'Sex work' works for pimps, pornographers and punters precisely because it doesn't make such lofty claims. It accords the trade a much lower profile, attempting to make it appear mundane, unremarkable, boring even.

And the more widely used the lexicon of 'sex work' is the better. Prompting people to reflexively use it through sheer force of familiarity, people who might not actually subscribe to the politics underpinning it upon analysis, is a marker of success. It's the tried and tested linguistic strategy of using conventional euphemisms to discourage people from actually engaging in that analysis.[54] As the euphemism that is 'sex work' takes root in everyday speech, its power to lobotomise listeners grows.

Not only does the labour frame camouflage the inherent sexual abuse, it also enables pimps, porn profiteers and brothel owners to go incognito. 'Sex workers can be employees, employers, or participate in a range of other work-related relationships,'[54] say NSWP. 'Sex worker' is a deliberately broad term. It is used to refer to pimps, brothel keepers, escort agency owners and pornographers ('employers'), in addition to those who actually participate in sex acts. 'Sex worker' collapses the widely differing roles and power relations within the trade into one inoffensive, media-friendly moniker.

A society that acts in law and language as if men who pay to sexually access women are simply consumers, legitmately availing workers of their services, is a society in deep denial about sexual abuse – and the sex inequality underpinning it.

MYTH 3: Porn is fantasy

'It was a studio in downtown LA and at first we didn't know what was going on,' Danny remembers. 'We just saw loads of men outside in their underwear and they sort of ran in. And we got in and there was all cameras, computers, wires everywhere, and two big rooms with sofas and posters of these porn stars. And suddenly the Porno Dan guy goes, "Welcome to *Fuck a Fan*."'

I spoke to twenty-four-year-old Danny Austin just over a year after he took part in a TV documentary about the pornography industry. It hadn't been his first time on a porn set. Danny had briefly been involved in the UK trade, performing in a total of six scenes after being approached via a dating website, aged eighteen, by a porn company. He'd soon decided he wanted out, though, having discovered drug use was endemic. 'I kept thinking, I don't want this to be where it leads me, I don't want to do this. So I stopped. I could see myself, if I continued, I probably would go down that road.' It was two years later when Danny spotted the call-out for men to participate in a British documentary called *Date My Porn Star*, which revolved around him and two other men travelling to Los Angeles to meet their favourite porn performers and to get a glimpse at the 'reality behind the fantasy' of the industry.[1] For Danny, it seemed too good an opportunity to pass up. 'I thought, oh it'd be a good idea to pick [the performer's] brain and see why he's still in the industry.' Which is how, in 2013, Danny Austin found himself standing near to Dan Leal – aka Porno Dan – looking on as the owner of Immoral Productions kicked off filming for *Fuck a Fan*.

To start, Leal set timed challenges for four assembled 'fans' who had successfully applied to take part in this porn film via the company's website. Three women hired by Immoral Productions were required to deliver the prizes. 'The person who got the lowest time just got a hand-job, the second from lowest would get a blow-job, third from lowest would get sex,' Danny recalls. 'But [Leal] said, "Fuck it, they can all fuck the girls." So this was about two o'clock in the afternoon, they started fucking the girls. It was basically just ongoing sex . . . Two o'clock in the afternoon probably until about twelve at night.' There were a few breaks from the filming, which was being live-streamed; 'like, water breaks, only for about twenty minutes and then they'd go back to it'. The British documentary included footage of one of the women in clear distress during the marathon porn shoot, while off-camera Danny noticed drugs playing a key role. Their purpose, it seemed obvious to him, was 'to dull the pain'.

During one of the breaks in the porn shoot, Leal explained to his UK visitors that many of the women hired for his porn films did escorting on the side. 'I noticed he would never call them by their real names or their stage names,' Danny told me. 'He would say "they" or "the girls" or "the bitches" or "the hoes". So he talked about them like they weren't really people.' Late into the night, the filming finally stopped. But Danny was horrified to discover that the women had to keep going, with Leal announcing it was now his crew's 'turn' with them. 'These girls had already been battered and chucked from one guy to another so they looked tired. I mean, the exhaustion on one of the girl's faces was like, oh my god . . . He loved what he was doing, which made it more disgusting for us to see. He loved what he was doing. It was awful.'

Danny was to get further insights into how Leal's firm functioned. The next day* the documentary team took him back to Immoral Productions to watch women audition for the company. 'I said, "I don't want to do this, this is disgusting, after what we saw last night."' But Danny's contract required him to go along and observe, so he and the other documentary subjects watched as a stream of women stripped naked for Dan Leal. 'He liked the young girls who weren't experienced at all . . . This one girl came in and she was like, "I've come to Hollywood to be a star, I wanna be an actress." And his eyes lit up.' Danny remembers Leal acting markedly different with the younger women. 'I think he preyed on young women . . . he was asking more questions: "Oh, have you ever had a boyfriend? Would you love to do porn?" Blah blah blah. And he was just very flirtatious with them: "Oh you're a pretty girl, you're a pretty girl, I bet you get told that all the time." Stuff like that. It was, like, kind of sick.' The women stripping for Leal that day were being cast for *Fuck a Fan*. But what stayed

---

* In the screened documentary, the visit to a porn set is shown before the filming of *Fuck a Fan*.

with Danny was just how quiet Leal was during casting on the subject of what the women were actually auditioning for. 'He didn't say what they would be doing. That's the bit that got me. And I don't think we were allowed to say that. He just basically said, "You'll be my star. I'll make you a star."

Appalled by what he witnessed in Los Angeles, Danny decided to speak out publicly after *Date My Porn Star* was screened in autumn 2013, which is how I came to interview him. The majority of women who appear in US-made pornography have filed through the casting rooms and studios of production companies in Los Angeles.[2] The footage these firms pump out now reaches a global audience of unprecedented magnitude, made possible by the accessibility, affordability, and anonymity of the transaction. This trio of consumer conditions, granted first by home video and, later, the internet, has helped create a cultural climate hospitable enough for pornographers to count another 'A' among their enablers: acceptability. The scale on which pornography is now consumed, overwhelmingly by heterosexual men and boys, strips away any pretences pornographers or porn watchers might once have had of representing a shunned 'counter-culture'. In England, 39 per cent of boys aged fourteen to seventeen regularly watch pornography, according to research conducted by a team from the universities of Central Lancashire and Bristol.[3] Dan Leal's personal brand of porn has seen him tread the increasingly well-worn path between pornography and mainstream media entertainment. His exploits were the focus of a 2012 documentary film, *Danland*,[4] and a reality TV series screened on Canada's Movie Central and The Movie Network, *The Right Hand.*[5]

And despite recurring claims that the growing glut of free online porn has caused the bottom to drop out of the pornography trade, the signs are that this is simply an industry changing, adapting. 'The days of making money in adult [entertainment] despite your own incompetence are well over,'[6] says Stephen Yagielowicz, from porn industry trade body, XBIZ. Sprawling firms such as MindGeek (previously Manwin) show there's still big money to be made, however. This porn conglomerate squeezes profits out of free porn sites like YouPorn through advertising revenue from pay-per-view sites,[7] while hoovering up production companies and 'niche' pornography sites into its asset fold. According to Yagielowicz, 'It's Las Vegas all over again: the independent owners, renegade mobsters and visionary entrepreneurs pushed aside by mega-corporations that saw a better way of doing things.'[8]

So, we have a lucrative and legally underpinned international trade in which profit-driven enterprises compete to push pornography onto people's screens and firmly into the bounds of what's deemed normal and acceptable. And yet, for all the earthly millions this trade ratchets up – in profits, in search engine results, in consumers – playing in the background is a narrative on loop: *porn isn't real, porn is fantasy.*

Ruminating about porn in the *Daily Mail*, commentator Toby Young maintains that for most men porn is nothing more than 'an escapist fantasy'.[9] Also drawing on this theme, The Site, billed as 'the online guide to life for 16–25 year-olds in the UK',[10] offers advice to young people about pornography on a page titled 'Porn vs reality': 'porn can be great',[11] it says. 'It's the idea that porn sex is like real sex which is the problem. But if you can separate the fantasy from the reality you're much more likely to enjoy both.'

Attempt to interrogate the footage turned out of pornography studios and its billing as 'fantasy', and you quickly find the notion that there is even a specific, identifiable 'thing' called pornography is contested. Despite LA's porn producers and their global audience seemingly having no trouble at all establishing a shared understanding of the word (when it's typed into Google, a highly distinct product that many millions readily consume is accessed), 'pornography' remains a remarkably slippery term. First of all, there's the multiple words competing for the same semantic space. Jostling with 'pornography' are the industry-favourite 'adult entertainment', the archaic legal category of 'obscenity', as well as the more sanguine sounding 'erotica'. Even when fixed on the word 'pornography', picking out a definition involves sieving through an assortment of interpretations and usages. UK law states 'an image is "pornographic" if it is of such a nature that it must reasonably be assumed to have been produced solely or principally for the purpose of sexual arousal',[12] making no reference to objectification, sex inequality, or harm in general. In contrast, a definition put forward by some legislatures in the US during the 1980s for material that qualified as legally actionable sex discrimination (and originally coined by feminist campaigners Andrea Dworkin and Catharine

MacKinnon) put it this way: 'Pornography shall mean the graphic sexually explicit subordination of women, whether in pictures or in words, that also includes one or more of the following,'[13] proceeding to catalogue six specific characteristics such as 'women are presented as sexual objects who enjoy pain or humiliation'. Then from this tightly defined point, 'pornography' is sometimes stretched so far as to be a by-word simply for things deemed sensual, indulgent or gratuitous, as in 'food porn' or 'poverty porn'.

But for all the varying ways that this word is thrown about in conversation and fixed in statute books, there is no question that 'pornography' in the twenty-first century is a term that is applied to a particular commercial practice, the most fitting description of which is implied by its root in ancient Greek: porné/pornos – meaning 'a woman for sale'/'a man for sale'.[14] It was a term for prostitution. 'Pornography' denotes a trade in which real, live women – not imaginary women, not fantasy women – are paid by companies like Porno Dan's to have sex at prescribed times, with prescribed people, for prescribed durations, in prescribed ways. Firms then peddle footage of this prostitution to a mass audience in order to turn a profit. Whatever else the word is used to describe, no one referring to 'pornography' in general terms today could seriously maintain that such a reference does not include the large-scale production, distribution and consumption of filmed prostitution. It is worth clarifying, then, that 'pornography' is used in this book primarily to refer to commercially produced images of the sexual objectification and/or sexual abuse of a person (usually a woman) for the sexual gratification of another (usually a man). This isn't an attempt to fix a universal definition. Because what's ultimately at stake here is not the integrity of abstract labels. What matters is the real, material harm experienced by women and girls as a result of a commercial trade in sexual access to women's bodies. And right now attempts to confront this harm are being obstructed by the myth that the pornography trade can be cordoned off as fantasy; the implication being that it doesn't affect *us* (or doesn't have to, as long as we learn to interpret it right), and there's no need for us to affect *it*.

So what precisely is it about the global pornography trade that prompts some people to frame it as within the realms of the imaginary?

Production

What definitely isn't imaginary about the pornography trade is the women who appear in porn films, the sex acts directors instruct them to perform, and the fact they are paid to be there. Nor is what this constitutes. 'Consent is a positive decision,'[15] insists youth website This Is Abuse; 'it's saying that you've decided you really want to have sex, each and every time . . . There are a million reasons why someone might not feel like having sex, e.g. a girl might be on her period, no condoms available, a person might have other things on their mind and not feel like it.' The bottom line, it says, is that if you are 'pressured into doing sexual things you don't like or aren't sure about, then this is abuse'.

If the pornography industry adhered to this guidance on preventing sexual abuse, production would grind to a halt.

Porn director Anna Arrowsmith unwittingly makes this apparent in her tips for would-be male and female performers. 'Be sure to ask producers/agents what exactly you will be expected to do on the day of the shoot,'[16] she recommends on her website. 'They should stick to the agreement, but so should you too!' The idea that people should have sex according to what they previously agreed, not according to how they feel at the time, falls rather spectacularly short of the 'positive decision' that constitutes consent. Another word of advice from Arrowsmith's site: appearing in porn requires 'perform[ing] acts you may not like doing'. So, perform sex acts you might not like, or don't get paid. I'd say that also comes up resolutely short.

When you watch standard porn industry produce, you are watching someone who had to be paid to be there; someone who wouldn't have got paid unless she turned up that day and unless she kept going until the scene was deemed 'finished' by the director; someone who is being instructed to perform particular sex acts; someone who is paid to respond during sex not according to how she really feels, but according to how the director and consumers want her to respond. You are watching documented evidence of a profit-driven industry that simply couldn't operate if the basic tenets of non-abusive sex were realised.

'Our objective is actually rather banal,' insisted Fabian Thylmann, founder of porn conglomerate Manwin, to journalists from Germany's *Financial Times*.[17] 'We want to create as many opportunities as possible for people to spend money.' Everything that takes place in a porn studio takes place in a wider market, and that market places porn producers in fierce competition with each other. Those unrelenting competitive pressures are brought to bear on pornographers, and thus on the women they pay to have sex in their films. It is this commercial setting that determines what happens in a porn film studio, not the sexual desires of the women being filmed. Pornography isn't fantasy – it's a corporeal trade that extracts profits from sexual abuse, fulfilling a demand that sex inequality created.

The pursuit of porn profits determines:

– what sex acts women are required to do (or, more accurately, endure)

In an article on AlterNet headlined 'Why I had to stop making hardcore porn', Sam Benjamin, who spent five years directing heterosexual porn films in LA, described his job like this: 'While my overt task at hand was to make sure that the girls got naked, my true responsibility as director was to make sure the girls got punished. Scenes that stuck out, and hence made more money, were those in which the female 'targets' were verbally degraded and sometimes physically humiliated.'[18] In a sexist society, where sex for a 'real man' entails sexually lording it over a woman, the biggest profits for pornographers lie in digging deeper into this misogyny. Throw in a relentless battle with other firms, open up a second front

against consumers' own tendency to habituate to porn images, and you have an industry dedicated to documenting and
ratcheting up the sexual abuse of women. Benjamin says,

> My various superiors across the years saw the issue from
> a businessman's perspective, reminding me quite openly
> of the need to keep up with our competition. Anabolic's*
> getting nasty? Then we need to be nastier . . . it almost
> seemed like an entire gender was being denigrated, like
> that was the whole point – where very young women
> were choked and slapped and written-on with lipstick,
> simply for the crime, it seemed, of being a woman. You
> should have slept with me, seemed to be the unspoken
> message. Now see what I have to do to you.

Another tactic some pornographers employ to up this deni-
gration is racism. Former porn performer Vanessa Belmond,
who was interviewed in the documentary *Date My Porn Star*,
has spoken out about her experiences of racism in the industry. Writing on the site antipornography.org, she recounts
being hired by the porn company producing a series called
Latina Abuse:

* Anabolic is an LA-based porn production company. A performer who
appeared in one of their past film series – *Rough Sex* – was quoted in the media
describing the experience: 'I got the shit kicked out of me . . . I was told before
the video – and they said this very proudly, mind you – that in this line most
of the girls start crying because they're hurting so bad . . . I couldn't breathe. I
was being hit and choked. I was really upset, and they didn't stop. They kept
filming. You can hear me say, "Turn the fucking camera off", and they kept
going.'[19]

One of the first things that the guy who picked me up told me was, 'You're lucky you're not working for Ghetto Gaggers (their black-themed site), we're meaner to the black girls.' What a relief! Don't get me wrong, they were still plenty 'abusive' towards me. I won't go into too much detail, but let's just say that after I was done with the shoot, I looked like I had been beaten up. I had red marks all over my body, and my eyes were so swollen that I looked like I had pink eye. Good thing they didn't cast me for the black site, because if they're meaner to black girls, I can only imagine how I would have looked (never mind FELT) after that! If that isn't racism, I don't know what is.[20]

The text description for the most recent film uploaded onto the *Latina Abuse* director's website when I visited it in April 2015 read:

Barato showed up to the Latina Throats studio with just the clothes on her back. This dumb whore couldn't even think of a stage name for herself. After learning that she only planned on doing this shoot and then she was done, no one was about to waste their precious time coming up with a sexy name for her. Thanks to the Spanish translation of the word 'cheap', this petite, five-foot, hundred-pound puta got her name. When it came time to take the cock down her throat, she tried to dodge them, but with a few crisp slaps she smartened up, swallowed the dicks then blew chunks all over. It's always the Latina whores who try to pull the over dramatic diva bullshit. Barato wasn't a fan of the pussy pounding either, but that didn't stop the guys from stretching her cunt out. I'm somehow glad that this was her first and last porn.

– when women have sex and with whom

There may well be 'a million reasons' why someone may not want to have sex on a particular occasion, but suffice to say, performer contracts handed out by porn production companies don't contain a million clauses allowing for this. Women are required to have sex on a pre-arranged day at a pre-arranged place at a pre-arranged time. So what happens if a woman turns up at a porn studio, as agreed, but finds when she gets there that she isn't attracted to the person (or people) she's having sex with, that she isn't in the mood and doesn't feel turned on, or that she doesn't like the sex acts the director is asking her to do? When there are camera operators waiting, sound and lighting technicians standing by, a director ready to start shooting, and a company that's financed this whole set-up, do you think she might feel under some pressure to have sex regardless of not wanting to? Do you think she would ever get hired if she turned up at porn sets and only went through with it when her desire to have sex happened to coincide remarkably precisely with the director's schedule? What was that advice about sex and pressure again?

Jessie described to me the acute stress she was put under while in the pornography industry:

It was always like a cycle of me getting sick, or another performer being sick and getting me sick. Because it's not like they don't work when they're sick. I tried to cancel a shoot before when I was really, really, really, really not feeling well and my agent basically made me go. And he was like, 'Companies would rather work with a sick girl than lose thousands of dollars.' And I was like, 'Are you serious?' So I went and I was like, 'OK fine, it's not going to be a good scene, and they probably won't make that much money off it.' And so I went and it was horrible.

Vanessa Belmond insists,

The vast majority of women in porn DON'T have much control over who they work with or for . . . There were some guys I didn't like working with, yet I still worked with them multiple times. If I had put all of those men on my 'no list' (the list of men women won't work with), it would have decreased my amount of work and therefore the amount of money I earned.[21]

– what women can say

At the start of some of her porn scenes directors would ask Jessie to do a faux interview on camera. It's a familiar feature of the footage turned out of pornography studios: the sooth-ing words reassuring viewers that the images they're mastur-bating to really needn't tweak their conscience. Everything's. Just. Fine. 'I would have a big smile on my face and be like, "I love porn. I wanna do this forever."' But Jessie pointed out to me that in practice there really wasn't an alternative. 'I did that because that was my business at the time. If I was in the porn industry and I told people actually I don't like this, I'm just doing it for the money, I wouldn't get booked and I wouldn't get fans. So that's really the reality of it.' Vanessa Bel-mond's description of doing interviews like this in the porn industry is almost identical. She writes:

> One of my favorite things to say when asked if I liked doing a particular scene was, 'I only do what I like! I wouldn't do it if I didn't like it!' (I would say this with a big fake smile and giggle.) What a total lie! I did what I had to do to get 'work' in porn. I did what I knew would help me gain 'fame' in the industry. Sure, technically I had a choice, I could always say no to a scene. But like most porn performers, I couldn't afford to turn down paying work, and I knew that if I said no too many times, my agent would stop calling. That's just a fact.[22]

The second-by-second feeling of genuinely wanting to con-tinue having sex with someone does not obey the contractual rules of the market. It's an emotional state dependent on hu-man relations, not a mechanism that can be switched on. It is also a feeling that can change at any point and so necessitates open communication. But that's rather more difficult if you have to follow a script or the only response that is acceptable to the director and viewer is affirmative.

– how long the footage can be viewed for

The year after I went along to the annual XBIZ pornography trade conference in London, journalist Amelia Gentleman paid a visit. One of the speakers she reported hearing was pornographer 'JT', who told the audience, 'Every two or three weeks we get a call from one of our performers, mainly in the Czech Republic, asking us to remove something. They say "My boyfriend will split up with me" or "He has taken my baby away". Some of them are really, really distressed.'[23] But the footage of these women having sex – which they do not want people to see – stays online. 'There is nothing we can do. The girls wanted to shoot, we pay them a lot of money . . .' ('JT' apparently clarified that 'a lot' actually translates to £314 for a four-hour session.) The fact that women in run-of-the-mill porn films don't get royalties is yet more proof for Jessie that the pornography trade is 'designed to screw the girl over whichever route she takes'. She told me that 'in reality porn is empowering for the man who creates the website and who is forever making money off those scenes, not for the girl shooting that scene one time and will never see that money.' In pornographer Anna Arrowsmith's handy list of tips for prospective performers she explains why the women porn companies pay to have sex on camera will have zero control over that footage: 'we sell the rights on to other companies'.[24] So, if you want to withdraw your permission for anyone with access to a computer being able to watch you having sex, legally speaking, tough. Pornographers' legal right to carry on making money from that footage currently trumps your right to take it down.

Maintaining that the pornography trade is not an industrialised form of sexual abuse relies on the fantastical notion that porn studios have somehow managed to create a kind of economic and sexual nirvana: a place where women's desire to have sex is miraculously in sync with the director's schedule; where she happens to want and like all the sexual acts required by the director and which just happen to be the sexual acts which are most profitable for said director; where women are given 'perfect information' before entering the industry and arriving at the studio and there are no negative consequences to backing out at any time; where there is zero coercion and pressure from agents, directors and production companies, and where they in turn are not ultimately beholden to market pressures. It's like an absurd parody of the neoclassical economist's wet dream of 'perfect competition, perfect information, and perfect rationality'.[25] 'People just really need to wake up about the reality of porn images,' Jessie insisted to me. 'It's not a fantasy. They're real human beings doing real things, and actually getting sick and getting hurt.'

Consumption

'Porn is a fantasy',[26] according to Planet Porn – a training resource for teachers, parents and anyone else who wants to broach the subject with young people. Activities include a card game where young players 'take it in turns to decide whether the statement belongs on "Planet Earth" (real life sex) or "Planet Porn" (porn sex)'.[27] The guidance explains, 'There are some things which porn teaches well and some things which porn teaches not so well'.[28] The implication is that if we visit Planet Porn we needn't bring anything harmful back with us to Planet Earth, so long as we know how to scan and decode the images. We just need to build a kind of porn customs in the mind: learn to let in the good, and filter out the hazardous. That way we can become discerning porn consumers and our notions of sexual consent and non-abusive sex on Planet Earth will remain blissfully uncontaminated. Any negative messages can remain in the realms of 'fantasy'. 'Think of porn as being like *Grand Theft Auto*,'[29] the resource advises. 'It's not real life'.

Wrong. Pornography isn't fantasy, it's proof. Proof to consumers that if your sexual desire for a woman isn't mutual, if she wouldn't gain sufficient sexual or emotional satisfaction from having sex with you, or for you, to do it for its own sake, then that's not necessarily a deal-breaker. She may be struggling to pay her rent! She might have racked up debts! In fact, we have an entire industry dedicated to engineering your (vicarious) sexual access to women who are only there on condition of payment.

Pornography is proof that society isn't altogether serious about the idea people should feel comfortable to communicate how they honestly feel during sex – without negative consequences. An industry in which women are paid *not* to communicate how they really feel during sex is free to operate.

Pornography is proof that right now society accepts and legally protects profits extracted from sexual abuse.

There is no way of neutralising this message from the pornography trade – the sense of entitlement it implies about gaining sexual gratification from a woman's body irrespective of how she really feels. To use pornography (and strip clubs and prostitution) is to use women as if they were instruments; mere tools for servicing sexual pleasure, not autonomous human beings whose own feelings, boundaries and desires are of equal concern.

Planet Porn *is* Planet Earth. There is no social vacuum separating us from the pornography trade. Prolific porn use primarily by heterosexual men and boys is evidence of cultural conditions prompting a major segment of the male population to feel able, willing and desiring of using women as dehumanised sex objects. The idea that somehow the powerful sexual reward they then receive while consuming this filmed prostitution has no bearing on their attitudes and behaviour, in a wider culture that echoes the message of male dominance, *is* fantasy.

Judging from the tenor of much of the public discussion surrounding the effects of consuming pornography, you could be forgiven for assuming that to roam through the archives of academic research on porn is to have to pick your way through a deeply confusing and uneven terrain, results strewn all over the place, making conclusions speculative and precariously balanced on highly subjective interpretations. That it requires selectively plucking out studies which back up said conclusion, whilst deliberately ignoring the rest (and hoping no one else notices them). Which is odd, given that the results from over four decades of academic enquiry into the effects of consuming porn are so resolutely stacked up on one side.

'The pornography trade fuels violence against women': against a backdrop of the full back-catalogue of research data on pornography's effects, this is an obvious statement. Move that statement into the public arena, however, and the academic rigour underpinning it – in fact, *demanding* this conclusion – is drowned out by a cacophony of conflicting claims. The dramatic mismatch between the data and the debate led Professor Catherine Itzin, previously co-director of the International Centre for the Study of Violence and Abuse at Sunderland University, to conclude that:

> Scientifically the situation for pornography and harm
> effects is similar to that of smoking and lung cancer. It
> is not possible to prove that smoking is the sole cause
> of the cancer, but there is sufficient correlational data
> to conclude that it is highly likely that smoking is a
> causal factor in the aetiology of lung cancer . . . Only the
> tobacco industry and its lobbyists still argue that there is
> no proof of a causal relationship.[30]

Firm conclusions either way about the overall effects of pornography consumption can't be drawn by wheeling out a single study, conducted by one set of researchers, with one set of participants, harnessing one methodology. Assessments on this scale rely on findings that are corroborated across methods, measures and samples – on the 'triangulation of data'. Join the dots between studies conducted inside and outside the lab, between a variety of sample groups, between quantitative and qualitative findings, and the picture that emerges is unmistakeable. 'The conclusions are robust and statistically significant',[31] observes Swedish researcher Dr Max Waltman, 'showing that consumption of pornography in all the forms typically demanded on the market causes gender-based violence as well as an array of attitudes that minimize, trivialize, or normalize it.' The effects have been shown to be 'significant, substantial, and independent of other causes.' Footage of women being used and presented as dehumanised sex objects, consumed while viewers enjoy the powerfully rewarding experience of sexual arousal and a masculinity-boosting sense of dominance, has a pretty unsurprising propagandising effect, influencing attitudes, beliefs and behaviours. *In the real world.*

Inconvenient and uncomfortable as the findings may be for some, here's a snapshot of what has been exposed through meta-analyses – a research method described as using 'statistical summarising techniques to provide an aggregation of existing evidence . . . This increases the sample size to a level from which it is possible to generalise from the findings obtained.'[32]

The finding: Exposure to pornography increases aggressive behaviour in the viewer.

The meta-analysis: Conducted by Allen, D'Alessio, and Brezgel (1995) using 30 experimental studies, involving 2011 participants in total.[33] Effect found for pornography depicting sexual activity classified as 'violent' and 'nonviolent'.

The finding: Consuming pornography increases viewers' acceptance of rape myths. (Myths like: 'a woman is partly responsible for being raped if she was wearing a short skirt at the time.')

The meta-analysis: Conducted by Allen et al., (1995) using 24 studies, involving 4,268 participants in total.[34] The association between exposure to porn and rape myth endorsement was revealed in experimental settings.

The finding: There is a significant association between using porn and holding attitudes supporting violence against women.

The meta-analysis: Conducted by Hald, Malamuth and Yuen (2010) using 9 non-experimental studies,[35] involving 2,309 participants in total. The types of attitude assessed in this meta-analysis predict sexually aggressive behaviours.

The finding: Exposure to pornography increases the risk of committing sexual offences.

The meta-analysis: Conducted by Oddone-Paolucci,

Genuis and Violato (2000), using 46 studies published between 1962 and 1995, involving 12,323 participants in total.[36] The researchers worked out that it would take a whopping 284 studies – as yet unreported – countering their finding for it to be dismissed as the consequence of mere sampling bias. As such, they conclude, 'the results of the meta-analysis are stable and generalizable' and 'the research in this area can move beyond the question of whether pornography has an influence on violence'.

In a kind of super-meta-analysis, Professors Catherine Itzin, Ann Taket and Liz Kelly reviewed five meta-analyses on the effects of using pornography.[37] Between them this added up to 124 separate studies, plus another 32 studies not featured in the meta-analyses. The review concluded that the effects of men's porn use include 'psychological desensitisation' leading to, for example, a lack of empathy with victims of rape and the belief that women actually enjoy rape; changes in attitudes, like buying into rape myths; and effects on behaviour, including being more likely to perpetrate aggressive acts. By triangulating findings from three decades of research into the effects of consuming pornography, the researchers were able to firmly conclude that 'taken together they constitute a substantial body of mutually corroborative evidence of the harm effects of extreme – and other – pornographic material'.

That's the top-line stuff, but the individual studies underpinning these conclusions offer an important glimpse at the plethora of scenarios in which pornography's pernicious influence plays out:

- Participants recommended a substantially shorter prison term for a man convicted of raping a woman who was hitchhiking after being exposed to pornography: five years – compared to the ten years recommended by those not shown pornography.[38]
- Men were significantly more likely to judge that a victim of 'date rape' experienced pleasure from the rape and 'got what she wanted' after watching an R-rated film (which was sexually objectifying, and not even sexually explicit).[39]
- Data collected between 2006 and 2010 revealed that women and men who watch pornography were more likely to oppose affirmative action for women in the workplace. (Importantly, though, opposition to affirmative action did not predict pornography use.)[40]
- Pornography use predicted a significant increase in men's self-reports of sexual aggression against women, independently of other factors, among a nationally representative sample of 3,000 young American men.[41]*
- Women participating in a support programme for victims of domestic violence were significantly more likely to have been sexually abused by their partner if he used pornography.[42]

* The biggest increase in self-reports of sexual aggression against women was observed among men classified as at 'high risk' of sexual aggression.

- Among a sample of nearly 500 eighteen- to twenty-nine-year-old heterosexual men, researchers found 'the more pornography a man watches, the more likely he was to use it during sex, request particular pornographic sex acts of his partner' and 'deliberately conjure images of pornography during sex to maintain arousal'.[43]

That the filmed prostitution peddled by porn studios inspires misogynistic beliefs and sexist violence isn't a hunch. It's not guesswork. It is the clear and consistent finding from over four decades of academic inquiry. The attitudes pornography inculcates and the accompanying feelings it elicits can foster a predisposition, as well as squash internal and external inhibitions, to perpetrating sexual abuse.

So, is all this to say that when it comes to using pornography, men react to porn with unlearned and uncontrollable acts of sexual aggression, much as psychologist Ivan Pavlov's dogs salivated when presented with food during his iconic experiment? A biological response so fundamental, so primal, that viewers could be conditioned to respond this way when they meet anyone who is, say, female? In a word: no.

Developing sexist beliefs and perpetrating violence against women is not a biological 'reflex'. It does not imply that if a man watches porn he *will* sexually coerce a woman. To use Catherine Itzin's earlier analogy, to say that smoking causes cancer is not to say that if you smoke you will get lung cancer. Nor is pointing to the influential role of pornography in the decision by some men to perpetrate sexual abuse to suggest that porn somehow operates in isolation – untouched by other factors or considerations. As the researchers who uncovered that porn use is associated with increased sexual aggression point out, 'no influence on human thinking or behavior works in a vacuum, and the influences of media combine and interact with a variety of other individual and cultural factors'.[44] As with any influence on people's actions in the world, porn's operation is complex – but its impact is clear. It is *a* – not *the*, not always in every case, but *a* – cause of attitudes and beliefs that endorse or trivialise violence against women, as well as corresponding acts of abuse themselves.

Analysis of the processes at play suggest pornography doesn't just stimulate sexual arousal, it stimulates a cognitive 'schema' – a mental framework for interpreting and responding to real-world action.[45] In practice it can function like a sexual script, guiding ideas and expectations in relation to sex itself. This was apparent in the study showing that the more men use pornography the more likely they are to ask their partner to engage in sex acts seen in porn.[46] It was also something that a group of sixteen- and seventeen-year-old boys I interviewed at their school were very conscious of. One of the boys remarked, 'If I said to someone that I watch porn, yeah, and I saw, like, a girl deep throat, I'll be like, "Ah yeah, you know what, yeah, I'm gonna try it on that girl." It's something you do. It's normal. It's normal. I think it's normal. I can't see anything wrong with it.'

Another student was more concerned about the implications. In his view, using pornography leads boys to 'think that women are very submissive and passive in the way they are about sex and stuff. 'Cause pornography creates a perception that women, like, it's degrading to the sex. They're animals that just have sex. They don't talk, they don't say no.' As this boy correctly alludes to, pornography can influence on a broader, collective level, shaping men's attitudes and behaviour not just in relation to an individual woman, but women in general. Because pornography teaches. Like any media it conveys values, knowledge, beliefs, *ideology*. The basic offering from this teacher is that women can engage in unwanted sex (i.e. sex for money) and have sex on demand, perform sex acts on the basis of external instruction in the absence of internal desire, react only in ways that please the director/ viewer rather than communicate how she really feels – *and that's OK*. The process of conveying this message (the porn production process) requires using and portraying individual women as indiscriminate sexual objects – degrading and dehumanising them as something akin to a real-life sex doll – which is then presented and experienced as sexually gratifying for the male consumer. The impact of watching pornography on men's levels of support for affirmative action is just one illustration of how, in the words of the study's authors, 'pornography activates an "abstract" script . . . antipathetic to women that influences a wider array of attitudes than those overtly displayed in pornography.'[47] This is dubbed pornography's 'carry over effect'. In short, you can't expect consumers to visit 'Planet Porn' – enjoy the sexual abuse and objectification of women – and then come back to Planet Earth and carry on as if it all just took place in a mental and emotional vacuum.

The significance of pornography as a driver of men's sexual violence is sometimes dismissed with the apparently earth-shattering observation that rape and sexual abuse pre-date the internet, and certainly pre-date the modern-day sex industry as we know it. Indeed they do. And what? The whole point about the concept of 'violence against women', what feminists have spent decades highlighting, is that the decision by some men to perpetrate this violence is not 'natural'. It is not somehow a part of men's essential nature. It is driven by sex inequality – by unequal societal power relations between women and men, underpinned by sexist attitudes, beliefs and practices (i.e. patriarchy). This in turn intersects with a host of other factors and forms of oppression, like racism, homophobia and economic inequality. The sexist, supremacist attitudes that underpin sexual violence do not spring from one single site. If that were the case, feminists would have been able to pack up their protests centuries ago. The attitudes leading some men to feel able, entitled, *desiring* to coerce or force a woman into sex flow from a multitude of coexisting sources. Some overt, some not. Some long since snuffed out (like the absence of legal penalties for rape*), some recently emerged. The pornography industry as we know it recently emerged. That does not disqualify it from posing a threat to women's safety. We live in a world where violence against

---

* It's worth noting, however, that a legal penalty for rape in marriage was only introduced in the UK as recently as 1991.

women is at epidemic levels. A US study published in 2013 found approximately one in four male university students reported having perpetrated sexual aggression. Over 10 per cent of them reported behaviour that met the legal definition of rape or attempted rape.[48] We are not so 'advanced' as a society, so utopian in our practice of sexual politics, that a significant propagandising force for violence against women could not emerge on our watch.

There is little question that in most mainstream heterosexual pornography, women are subjected to overt aggression. But that doesn't mean concern over its effects can simply be filed away amongst the contentious debates surrounding the effects of viewing violence more generally. The fact that aggression towards women in pornography is communicated through sexual acts, while the viewer masturbates, is not somehow incidental. Reviewing data on its effects, Professor Neil Malamuth noted that 'when a message is presented within a sexually explicit context, it may have different effects than when presented in a nonexplicit context, because the content is perceived differently and because arousal is generated'.[49] Sexual arousal acts to powerfully reinforce the messages that porn propagates.

Crucially, it's not just pornography classed by researchers as overtly violent that produces the real-world effects I've outlined here. In fact, Dr Max Waltman cites evidence that 'violent materials might not affect sexually aggressive behaviors among every individual as strongly as dehumanizing nonviolent materials do'.[50] So the fact that women in pornography are required to perform as if they were living sex dolls – free of boundaries, negative responses and an off switch – is central to the distorting effect it has on users' attitudes and actions. It fuels the belief in male entitlement to sex on demand; a solipsistic attitude that fails to acknowledge, for instance, the 'million reasons why someone might not feel like having sex'. It is an attitude that fails to acknowledge the full humanity of women.

The pornography trade is politically toxic for the social status of women and girls. The sexual abuse and objectification inherent to commercial production is central to the experience of consumption. Watching pornography boils down to watching filmed prostitution – to commercial sexual exploitation. To use this footage as a masturbation aid involves either being OK with that exploitation, trivialising it, or – perhaps just as frighteningly – not seeing it.

Yeah, but . . .

. . . don't worry about it. Really, if that all sounds like a bit of a downer, there's absolutely no need to, you know, do anything about it. If you're one of those who's bothered by a commercial trade predicated on the sexual abuse and objectification of women, if a profit-driven industry recycling inequality between women and men gives you cause for concern, *relax*. Apparently.

See, there's now porn that's directed by women. And porn that's walking off with prizes at the Feminist Porn Awards!

Speaking to *Salon*, Tristan Taormino, who co-edited *The Feminist Porn Book*, said,

> Every day, someone writes to me and says, 'OK, I just found out there's this thing called feminist porn.' That's super-exciting because I feel like it shifts the dialogue; the next time that a friend of that person says, 'God I hate porn,' they can turn to them and say, 'Have you seen all the porn that's out there? Because I don't know if you have, and there are alternatives.'[51]

Isn't that great, how we can now divert the focus of people concerned about the pornography industry? Former porn site operator and industry advocate Jerry Barnett is equally cheered by the trend. He writes approvingly that 'increasing numbers of feminist porn directors, instead of attacking the medium, have set out to improve it'.[52]

A tiny subsection of the pornography trade – porn directed by women, porn branded 'feminist' – is being proffered up as a response to industry condemnation, managing to reframe concerns about porn as concerns about 'bad porn', while *in no way undermining the trade's fundamental medium of filmed prostitution*. This isn't a threat to the pornography trade. It's a gift. And the idea that it's any kind of 'solution' to the sexual abuse and objectification inherent to the trade *is* pure fantasy.

'What women need is women pornographers who can help create new images that will build a liberating feminist sexuality'[53] – not a recent take on the issue, but a characterisa-

tion by researchers of a position pushed during porn debates
in the 1980s. Yet recent analysis of pornography films directed by women punctures the inflated feminist credentials ac-
corded them. In a study published in 2008, US researchers
assessed 122 scenes from 44 top-renting pornographic films,
half directed by men, half by women.[54] The female-directed
films were just as violent as those directed by their male coun-
terparts. Their scenes contained an equal average number of
aggressive acts in over three-quarters of the scenes, including
choking, slapping and gagging. 'Ass-to-mouth' was present
in 41 per cent of female-directed scenes and 44 per cent of
male-directed scenes. The targets of over 90 per cent of this
aggression were the same: women.[55] Also the same was how
women were shown responding: 97 per cent of the aggressive acts perpetrated in both male- and female-directed porn
were met by the target with either a neutral or pleasurable expression. The message, then, remained consistent, regardless
of who was directing: women don't mind sexual aggression
against them. In fact, they like it.

A contrast that did emerge, however, was the likelihood
that women would participate in violence against other wom-
en. Female-directed pornography was substantially more likely to feature a woman as the perpetrator of aggression against
another woman. In such a competitive, male-dominated market, the researchers reflected on female pornographers, 'How
best to demonstrate one's allegiance to patriarchy, thereby
increasing one's status, than to exhibit one's masculinity by
severely violating another woman?'[56] Ultimately, they con-

cluded, 'Money, rather than gender, dictates vision.' Male and female pornographers serve the same bottom line. Much as the industry would be delighted if their customer base expanded, the reality is that demand for filmed prostitution, for footage that sexually objectifies, overwhelmingly comes from heterosexual men. And that demand is midwifed by sex inequality, by misogyny. The most profitable pornography inevitably reflects this, regardless of who's directing.

Notwithstanding who's behind the camera, Tristan Taormino says on her website that 'there is no easy answer to the question, "What is feminist porn?" because there is no singular definition of feminist porn, but rather multiple ideas and definitions.'[57] As well as running her own porn company, Taormino openly cites her role as an 'exclusive director' for mainstream, LA-based pornography producer, Vivid Entertainment (reported by Forbes in 2005 to generate an annual revenue of $100 million[58]), as well as writing an 'advice column' for one of Larry Flynt's porn magazines, *Hustler's Taboo*.[59] Taormino told *Cosmopolitan* magazine, 'Feminist porn seeks to empower the performers who make it and the people who watch it . . . I call feminist porn "organic, fair trade porn" and liken it to the organic and fair trade movement in the United States.'[60]

Yet the judging criteria for films submitted to the Feminist Porn Awards, an annual event run by a Toronto-based sex shop, are somewhat more vague on what qualifies as 'feminist porn' than might be implied by comparisons to the Fairtrade certificate, and the precise standards that imposes. The four criteria used to assess films at the Awards are: '*Quality* – We love to award films that look great. We believe it is possible to make a great-looking film even with a limited amount of resources . . .'; '*Inclusiveness* – We recognize in a niche-based industry like porn not all films are for all audiences and aren't able to include everyone. But we also love it when films make an effort to explore sexualities that are often marginalized or ignored by mainstream porn . . . It's our goal to highlight and celebrate films that appeal to a diversity of audiences . . .'; '*The 'it' factor:* Movies that showcase a unique perspective are especially appealing, whether this is about the story being told, the interactions between characters or technical aspects like framing and editing . . .'; and finally, '*Hotness:* Bodies are well-lit, framed and shot to perfection, desire radiates off the screen, and all parties involved appear enthusiastic. Plenty of orgasms don't hurt either!'[61]

Somewhat hazy definitions aside, how has the mainstream industry responded to this supposed upstart? If there's a new pornography positioning itself as the 'feminist' version, that rather casts aspersions over the rest of the trade – implying it is sexist, regressive, *not feminist*. So, has it managed to kick off a revolution in the porn world or have the big players gone out gunning for the new pretender – ridiculing it, smearing it?

Neither, actually. The 2014 XBIZ Awards, the annual 'Oscars of porn',[62] offered a telling display of this. That year Porno Dan's company, Immoral Productions, received nine award nominations for series including *Fuck a Fan Global Edition 1* and *Titterific* – promoted with the tag line, 'If you're a breast man you can't miss this one! We're groping, grabbing and sucking on the most impressive racks in the business!'[63]* At some point during the ceremony, in among handing out gongs for Hustler Video's *Busty Beauties Car Wash* and *The Hooker Experience* by Evil Angel (a company which boasts being 'the leaders in gonzo porn and hardcore anal sex videos' and produces series such as *Asian Anal Assault* and *Watch Me, Bitch*), XBIZ neatly slotted in a new award amongst their 151 other award categories: Feminist Porn Release of the Year.[64]

So-called 'feminist porn' isn't a foe of the mainstream industry, it's a friend. Financially, it's a brand that could help expand the consumer base, hooking in customers who might previously have felt a bit awkward clicking on *Watch Me, Bitch*, for instance. Politically, as a brand, it's an alibi. As Taormino highlighted, now when people say 'I hate porn' or, god forbid, try and do anything to infringe on the profit-making pursuits of pornographers, this particular niche can be wheeled to the front of the stage as if to say, 'Look, we're not all bad and, hey, if you watch more of this stuff you'll be upping the demand for it and really making a difference.' This category of pornography can play a 'feministwashing' role for the industry *because it's pornography*; because it doesn't challenge the inherently sexually abusive mode of production but does reinforce the myth that sexual consent is a commodity. Which is all very useful for the likes of Hustler and Evil Angel, thank you very much.

---

* Porno Dan didn't actually win anything that year at the XBIZ Awards. Bless.

The idea that this could ever be some kind of solution even to the most overtly misogynistic and degrading footage turned out of porn studios, that it could be a 'game-changer', rather presupposes that the millions of men and boys currently generating profits by masturbating to the likes of *Asian Anal Assault* simply haven't stumbled across feministporndotcom yet. Which both puts a whole lot of faith in the power of the free market to sort out this spanner in the feminist project and, regarding present porn consumer habits, is naive at best. As I've highlighted, the habituation effects of using pornography drive consumption preferences in the opposite direction: towards content that is more violent, more degrading. And it will continue to, until the porn industry stops being given a free pass as 'fantasy' and is instead confronted by a real challenge: a challenge to the licence society currently grants pornographers like Porno Dan to pursue profits from filmed prostitution.

MYTH 4: Objecting to the sex trade makes you a pearl-clutching, sexually conservative prude

An attractive woman in a bikini [is] not the source of all evil as is claimed by what is basically a minority group of fanatical fundamentalist feminists.

PIERS HERNU, former editor of Front magazine[1]

The anti-prostitution lobby makes little or no distinction between sex work in which prostitutes retain a measure of agency and sex trafficking – modern slavery. This is because it's the 'sex' part of those activities that really causes knickers to be twisted in the icy corridors of bourgeois moral opprobrium.

LAURIE PENNY, commentator, writing in the New Statesman[2]

FACILITATOR: . . . get the group to think about how you could turn their interests into your interests. For example . . . how could you tarnish their image? Be as creative as you like and, at this stage don't allow feasibility to hold you back.

Group exercise from a campaign guide on how to challenge the 'Swedish model' of prostitution (an approach which recognises prostitution as violence against women)[3]

Are your knickers in a twist yet? Mine are so twisted from writing this it's like wearing cheese wire. But then, I did read in the scriptures of fanatical fundamentalist feminism that this is a penance that should be endured. So that's some comfort, I guess.

Imaginary lingerie upsets aside, here we come to a different kind of myth. Unfortunately for its fans, rehashing fairy tales about the nature of the sex trade isn't a sufficient bulwark against opposition. When the trade's kernel of sexual abuse and objectification is properly exposed, a lot of people tend to notice its incompatibility with basic notions like humanity and equality. Which is why it is also necessary to peddle myths about the people pointing this out. Why it's necessary to 'tarnish their image'. This is where the gloves come off and the myth-making gets unabashedly personal.

The objective is simple: frighten people off speaking out against the sex trade, and undermine those that do. Fear and smear – it's a hardly a new tactic. It can, however, be an effective one.

The prospect of being targeted by sex trade advocates who deal with detractors in this way is one of the main reasons 'Marie', who was involved in Germany's prostitution trade, won't use her real name and appears in disguise when speaking in public about her experiences. 'I need to do it anonymously because I think that there will be hate they put on me and experience in other countries shows me that this will happen.' Tanja Rahm does feel able to reveal her identity when talking about her time in the Danish prostitution trade, but says 'going out in public isn't easy'. She told me that you have to be 'able to ignore the hate you meet . . . In Denmark we are actually quite many who have been out public, telling about our experiences from prostitution, but a lot of them gets threatened and silenced by women-haters [and] the pro-[prostitution] lobby.'

Crystal, who was exploited through prostitution in the UK, is all too aware of these silencing tactics. 'The hostility of the pro-prostitution lobby is unrivalled,' she told me. 'It has been probably the key driver in my decision to remain anonymous in my blog, my writing and speaking. I've seen other survivors of prostitution who have written openly and honestly how prostitution has damaged them be completely trashed and taken to the cleaners. The attacks are both brutal and personal – deeply personal. They have been called mentally ill, liars, man haters.' Despite not revealing her identity, Crystal has nonetheless been on the receiving end of abusive comments via her online writing:

> They have varied from telling me to shut the fuck up, that I'm a man hater and deserve to be dead, to saying they are getting off on the abuse I've described and they're looking forward to perpetrating it on their 'girlfriend', to saying it couldn't have been that bad or I would have left. The comments vary but the tone, the frightening hostility, does not. It's not pleasant – an understatement of course – to get comments like that anyway without people coming after me in person. So I remain anonymous.

Acknowledging the pivotal role of fear and smear tactics in shielding the sex trade from political opposition is not to imply that there is no such thing as a bad argument against the trade. Of course there is. Whether it be ignorant and prejudiced judgments about people paid for sex to conservative proscriptions about sexual relationships, it should go without question that these are chucked on the political garbage heap. They have nothing to do with ending violence, nothing to do with promoting equality. But feminist objections do. Feminist opposition to the sex trade is unequivocally rooted in recognition of the sexual objectification and abuse at the core of this phenomenon, as well as the harms meted out to all women and girls as it becomes embedded in society.

The campaign guide cited at the start of this chapter on how to oppose the 'Swedish model' of prostitution, published by an Amsterdam-based group called International Committee on the Rights of Sex Workers in Europe, contains this note of caution for readers: 'Danger Points: Look out for your opponent's killer response. They may employ a public relations (PR) firm and will try and sell the message of how prostitution is violence against women. Prepare your counter attack.'[4]

When it comes to countering opponents, the guide is rather short on examples of how to 'tarnish their image'. So if you're not feeling very 'creative', if the challenge of defending a commercial market in sexual abuse doesn't yet inspire you into enthusiastic rhetorical flurries, fear not. Below are a few suggestions to get you started. Then if you do happen to stumble across anyone hateful or ignorant enough to suggest that the industrialisation of sexual exploitation should be curbed, you'll know just how to respond.

MYTH 4

What to say: 'If you're opposed to the sex trade that means you must be opposed to sex itself. Eurgh, look at you, with your twin set and pearls, your chastity belt and your legs bolted together.'*

*Don't worry about your sartorial observations being completely made up. Just let your imagination run. Really go for it! In fact, don't credit your opponent with even being able to utter words like *sex* or *pornography*. Instead, when attributing opinions to these loathsome objectors, try using terms dripping with conservative condemnation, like *smut, indecency* and *filth*. That should help get your message across. Building from there, try conjuring up the spectre of an actual conservative crusader (dead or alive, doesn't matter) who forecasts fire and brimstone for any sexual relationship that is non-procreative and outside the bounds of marriage and a heterosexual nuclear family. Then, just tar the feminist objectors by association. It doesn't matter that their views and values are diametrically opposed to said spectre; that's the beauty of this logical fallacy. Merely mentioning them in the same sentence will get your smear campaign off to a healthy start.

Jerry Barnett, who was dubbed by the BBC in 2008 as 'boss of the UK's biggest adult website', has got the hang of this tactic.[5] Writing on the Feminist and Women's Studies Association website, he notes that by the time social conservative campaigner Mary Whitehouse died in 2001, her 'anti-permissiveness' agenda was 'a target for mockery rather than widespread support'.[6] Indeed. But then in a deft move,

Barnett alleges that this 'did not mean that anti-sex morality had died'. Instead, 'the morality movement regrouped, using MacDworkinite feminist language and ideas, and presented itself as a women's rights movement, rather than a moralistic one'. Brilliant. Don't just associate, say they're one and the same! In case anyone should be left wondering exactly who these modern-day Mary Whitehouses are, Barnett helpfully clarifies by bestowing the title of 'leading anti-sex feminist groups in Britain today' on Object and UK Feminista, in honour of their opposition to the strip-club, porn and prostitution industries.

Finally, to really cement the myth that feminists opposing the sex industry are actually the Junior Anti-Sex League incarnate, summon up its notional opposite. Barnett again: 'Sex-positive feminism is perhaps as strong as ever',[7] he reassures his readers. See, if you can get the claim past people that endorsing prostitution, porn and strip clubs is 'sex-positive', you backhandedly boost the idea of its opposite.

Don't mention: that labelling feminist opposition to the sex trade 'anti-sex' is about as logical as saying that anyone who agrees votes shouldn't be for sale is 'anti-voting' or that opposing a commercial trade in human organs means you must be anti-organ replacement. Jennifer Hayashi Danns, author of the book *Stripped: The Bare Reality of Lap Dancing*, told me 'the idea that the sex industry is sex-positive and liberal [is] an absolute joke' and that lap-dancing clubs like the one she used to work in are 'just a manifestation of gender inequality'. So, probably best not to quote her then. And definitely don't acknowledge that branding your opponent anti-sex is a hackneyed misogynistic slur designed to shame and humiliate feminist objectors, or that the 'anti's which do accurately sum up their beef with brothels, porn sets and lap-dancing clubs are in fact anti-sexism, anti-sexual abuse and anti-sexual objectification.

What to say: 'Call yourselves feminists? No one's holding a gun to the heads of women in strip clubs, porn sets and brothels (well, not to most of them anyway). You're denying their agency and turning them into helpless victims* – so you can't be a feminist after all, can you.'

*When uttering the word 'victim', try sneering as you say it. This will help emphasise that you are using the word as a pejorative and implying that when somebody decides to perpetrate harm against another person, it's somehow shameful for the person who is the target of their abuse. That to be a victim would somehow be embarrassing, a sign of weakness perhaps, rather than a sign of the perpetrator's hateful attitudes. The trick here is that if you can deny that there are any 'victims' (always use scare quotes) then there can't be any perpetrators. And if there aren't any perpetrators then there can't be any abuse, and then the whole sex trade can carry on just as it was, thank you very much. *And,* if anyone's making women in the trade into victims, it's the industry's opponents who are casting them as such. (See how you can pass the buck for perpetrating harm from the men who pay to sexually access women's bodies to the feminists pointing this out? Neat, huh?)

Again, you can always build on this theme. Like by implying that it's not possible to exercise autonomy, make decisions or take steps to manage a situation in which people are perpetrating harm against you. Basically, this boils down to, 'unless you are a robot or someone's holding a knife to your throat, you wouldn't remain in an abusive situation, that it's insulting to suggest otherwise, that it would be to deny a person's *agency*'. Attribute the phrase 'false consciousness' to your opponent now and again (doesn't matter that they didn't actually say it) and make them seem really insulting and patronising. Yeah!

Don't mention: that nine out of ten people involved in prostitution report wanting to use their 'agency' to leave the trade, but feel unable to do so.[8] Also try not to mention that there are women around the world who have been exploited through the sex trade and are speaking out against it, often at great emotional cost. Women such as Crystal, who maintains that 'to be opposed to the sex trade is to stand alongside women like me, who it has chewed up and spat out, to listen to us, to take our stories seriously. It is to refuse to listen to the lies of the sex industry. It is to say, "I judge the johns – not the women they use".' In fact, probably best not to even attempt this particular smear tactic if the sex trade opponents you are confronting have been involved in the trade themselves – it doesn't tend to work as well. And best not to roll out the phrase 'listen to sex workers' as short-hand for 'stop criticising the sex industry', otherwise you will have just inferred they don't exist. Or don't count.

The tricky balancing act involved in (mis)using the concept of agency as a trump card in defence of the sex industry, while also discounting women who have experienced the trade and are exhibiting 'agency' through campaigning to abolish it, is neatly illustrated by the Red Umbrella Fund. This global money pot, hosted by women's rights funder Mama Cash, says it exists to 'strengthen and ensure the sustainability of the sex worker rights movement.'[9] In a section titled 'our values and operating principles' on the fund's website, the top two principles that apparently guide their allocation of grants are: 'We recognise the self-determination of sex workers' and 'We believe that sex workers must be at the heart of the design, implementation, and evaluation of programs.'[10] But then there's the third principle: 'We oppose the criminalisation of sex work and recognise that sex work is work.' Right. So that's financial backing for your self-determination unless you recognise your experiences as sexual abuse, not 'work', and/or oppose the decriminalisation of brothel-keeping and pimping. Best to avoid articulating something as thoroughly reprehensible as this so openly when trying to silence feminist opposition to the sex trade. Although, if you are dishing out money this puts you in a more powerful position to the groups concerned so it might not be a massive problem.

Another thing not to bring up when confronting those opposed to the sex trade: the clear and important parallels this issue has with domestic violence, where public debates have long been dominated by questions like, 'if he's really so abusive, then why doesn't she leave?' What survivors and campaigners have spent decades highlighting is that exercising 'agency' – i.e. remaining in an abusive relationship without having to be locked in a room twenty-four hours a day – is entirely consistent with the partner's behaviour continuing to be deeply harmful; that the emotional and psychological barriers to getting away can be immense, as can the practical ones – like finances, the risk of reprisal for leaving, or just having somewhere else to go.

What feminists have shown is that it is not only possible but a fundamental imperative to understand and respect a woman's methods of dealing with abuse while at the same time not excusing the perpetrator and simply ignoring the danger he poses, nor ignoring the grave problem of domestic violence on a societal level. It's about unequivocally recognising that the behaviour of domestic violence perpetrators is oppressive, abusive, sexist – *and* that those subjected to it can and do respond to it in different ways, for a multitude of reasons. Conflating opposition to the sex trade with a wholesale denial of women's autonomy and the possibility there may be a multiplicity of experiences and reactions within the trade is total bunkum. So attempts to discredit feminist opponents of the industry would benefit from not drawing attention to the fact that this particular smear just hands pornographers, pimps and punters a get-out-of-jail-free card.

Jennifer Hayashi Danns told me that she wrote *Stripped*, her book about the lap-dancing club industry, as 'an intentional antithesis to the status quo, which I perceive to be that the sex industry is a harmless, liberal, normal industry that provides a valuable service'. Yet she explained that while she was still performing, 'I would say that it hadn't affected me at all, and that I liked my job as it gave me the freedom to complete my university studies and be independent'. Why? Because at the time, she says, 'you don't have the luxury of introspection. You would go mad and then lose your source of income. You may have changed your mind, but your bills will have stayed the same and are not going to pay themselves.'

A couple of extra points to be aware of: as a cause and consequence of sex inequality, and a market unavoidably intertwined with the rest of society, the sex trade affects all women and girls, so just zooming in on (and misrepresenting) the concept of agency for those directly involved won't cut it. And to imply that recognising a perpetrator has committed abuse and thereby *victimised* a woman is somehow a slight on the woman, that the term 'victim' is a pejorative, is contemptible victim-blaming. It's an experience all too familiar to Marie, who decided to enter the prostitution trade after struggling to find a job near enough her home in Germany. 'I really didn't want to go on welfare that time,' Marie told me. 'The last option, legal option, was to sell myself . . . I said, "OK, I have to do something. I'm a grown-up woman. I'm a strong woman." I like sex, always liked sex. I don't have a relationship so I had one-night stands, things like that. I enjoyed it. So I said "OK, it's nothing different. Maybe I can do that."' But despite the German state categorising prostitution as an ordinary job, Marie says she was 'traumatised by all the experiences I made . . . I lost many things and it affects me still. And I don't know whether it will change or not.' Yet since speaking out about her experiences of sexual abuse, Marie has repeatedly faced a disturbing response. 'How often did I hear now the words, "I am so sorry for you that you were not strong enough to do this job". No! No woman is "not strong enough" for the job. It is not her weakness which makes this trade harmful for her!'

What to say: 'This is nothing but a moral panic.'*

*While saying this, try to imagine you are a member of a clandestine avant-garde cell, courageously fighting for the enlightened few against a giant hysterical blob of mindless busybodies.

Don't mention: that the Oxford Dictionaries definition of 'moral' is 'Concerned with the principles of right and wrong behaviour'.[11] Other common terms for this include ethics, ideals and values. So if you're relying on the 'moral' bit of your slur to shut down feminist opposition, it's a bit like saying, 'Look at you with your ethics, thinking it's a bad thing to cause harm to another human being, to materially disadvantage them, to treat them as if they are inherently subordinate to you. How *embarrassing!*'

As for the 'panic' bit, implying opposition to the sex trade is little more than fevered delirium, long since severed from logic, research or evidence, well, take a look at the rest of this book. And then probably ignore it. Same goes for initiatives like SPACE International – an organisation run by sex trade survivors which 'is committed both to raising the public's consciousness of the harm of prostitution and to lobbying governments to do something about it.'[12] Rachel Moran, who was exploited in prostitution and who co-founded SPACE International, says, 'There is nothing panicked about our opposition to the sex-trade. It is deliberate, organised and determined. As for moral, I have no problem being moral, being ethical and in doing so calling for the liberation of those who are commercially sexually exploited under oppressive economic, social and racial systems.'

What to say: 'Simply campaigning to abolish the sex trade is too negative. What's your positive alternative?* It's also a divisive issue. Is that what you want to do, divide? Oh, by the way, as this headline put it, "The '80s called and they want their sex wars back".[13] **

*What you're trying to do here is create the impression that it's not commercial sexual exploitation that's the downer we should be focusing on, it's the party-poopers pointing it out. Suggesting your opponent should come up with an 'alternative' can also helpfully imply that brothels, porn sets and strip clubs are a *solution* to something, and that if you do away with them you'd better have something else lined up. Journalist Toby Young, for instance, bemoans feminist 'bluestockings'[14] who yack on about how porn objectifies women. Young reassures readers that he 'learned far more about the birds and the bees from reading the letters in Penthouse' than he did at school, and that it's 'surely far better that sex-starved husbands should satisfy themselves by watching a couple of blue movies than straying from the nest and looking for real-life partners.'

**Try drawing on historical debates and narratives to pigeon-hole protesters of commercial sexual exploitation (or 'fanatical fundamentalist handkerchief-clutching do-gooders' as you should now be calling them) as stuck in the past. A dangerous past. A past that threatens to eat feminism. Insisting that feminism during the 1980s was marked by calamitous 'sex wars' will simultaneously reinforce the myth that sex industry opponents were and are arguing against sex, not sexual objectification, while usefully reframing the struggle as being feminist vs feminist, rather than feminist vs pimp/pornographer/punter.

Basically, to shut down opposition, the key message to communicate is that it's not a multi-billion dollar global industry dedicated to the sexual abuse and objectification of women that poses an existential threat to women's equality. It's feminists. Feminists who just won't agree to disagree on the question of whether strip-club owners, porn producers and brothel keepers are entrepreneurs or exploiters. Imply that if they would only get off their hobby-horse and pitch in with the *real* business of busting patriarchy then we could probably get the whole thing sewn up within the month. Or at least within the year. Take heart from the fact that the status quo is on your side: if society does agree to park the issue because it's seen as too controversial (note: make every effort to ensure that it is controversial) then it's business as usual for the sex industry.

Here's an extra line you could use: 'This debate is feminism's *Groundhog Day*. It's little more than a tired re-run and, well, frankly your objections to the sex trade are futile. Don't bother resurrecting a polarised past, there's no need! We've found a third way: a reasonable, nuanced middle ground.' It doesn't really matter what you sell this middle ground as exactly, just as long as it allows for the preservation of a market based around men paying to treat women as sex objects. *The Economist* conjured up a 'reasonable middle' to place itself in when it urged governments in 2014 to abandon efforts to abolish the sex trade: 'NIMBYs make common cause with puritans, who think that women selling sex are sinners, and do-gooders, who think they are victims. The reality is more nuanced. Some prostitutes do indeed suffer from trafficking, exploitation or violence; their abusers ought to end up in jail for their crimes. But for many, both male and female, sex work is just that: work.'[15] The then editor of *FHM*, Ross Brown, tried this tack when questioned by journalist Janice Turner. Brown's 'third way' defence of his magazine's sexual objectification of women was to claim he had discovered a special kind of sexism: non-sexist sexism. 'There is at times a huge sliver of sexism in *FHM* – of course there is,'[16] he said. 'We do it because our readers laugh at it.' Similarly, Phil Hilton, then editor of lads' mag *Nuts*, dismissed Turner's suggestion that the pornified pictures in his magazine were a misogynistic throwback. 'You are imposing outmoded sexual politics on a world that doesn't fit any more.'

Don't mention: that sexual abuse and objectification are a solution to nothing. To call for the abolition of the sex trade is to call for a world in which women and girls are seen and treated as equals to men and boys, not as subordinate sex objects. It's to call for a world where we recognise that sexual consent doesn't run on a meter, and whether the person you have sex with actually wants to have sex with you isn't an optional extra. To even attempt to brand this as 'sex negative', as leaving a void that requires a ready packaged alternative to fill it, is to imply that misogyny is integral to sex. And that, ironically, is an astonishingly negative view of sex. As the legal scholar Professor Catharine MacKinnon reflects, 'to consider "no more rape" as only negative, no more than an absence, shows a real failure of imagination'.[17]

Best not to let on that this debate isn't *feminism's* problem, either. Feminism is a broad-based global movement of people, ideas, actions: not a cult. The absence of total uniformity amongst all those who proclaim themselves committed to its aim will not bring the whole thing crashing down. What the existence of feminist opposition to the sex trade *is* a problem for is the sex trade. In a society where people are, for the most part, signed up to the notion that women and men should live as equals, the endurance of a commercial trade dedicated to the sexual objectification of women depends upon the construction of an elaborate fairy tale – a Neverland where men have uncontrollable sexual urges, where the experience of serving a customer his chosen drink is comparable to performing his chosen sex act on him, and where there's nothing anyone can do about it anyway. When people start pointing out that this is pure fantasy is when the trade's foundations begin to crumble.

If trying the 'it's so polarised, here's my reasonable middle ground' approach, try to avoid discussion of basic logic. To illustrate: if one person argues that women are always to blame for being raped, and another person argues that it is never a woman's fault if she is raped, the 'compromise position' – that women are sometimes to blame for being raped – does not somehow acquire any credibility whatsoever by virtue of just being the middle ground between two positions. Applied here: 'the sex trade is inherently harmful' + 'the sex industry is inherently benign' ≠ 'the existence of the sex trade *can* be harmful, but not always'.

Finally, if the mud you're slinging at feminists just won't stick, if they keep blathering on about how a trade based on sexual abuse and objectification is bad blah blah blah, then you can always go back to basics and deride their appearance – like *Hustler* founder Larry Flynt when he took on US feminist icon Gloria Steinem, insisting '[her] only claim to fame is urging some ugly women to march'.[18] And, frankly, could there be anything more personally devastating than being told by a strip-club-owning, hardcore-porn-producing publisher of *Barely Legal* magazine that he doesn't find you attractive?

MYTH 5: Decriminalise the entire prostitution trade and you make women safe

'I often think I'm perhaps ready to hang up my "struggle" T-shirt.' South African activist Nozizwe Madlala-Routledge laughs, self-deprecatingly. 'But every time I think no, I can't. I can't hang it up because we are not free yet.' I met Madlala-Routledge in the Cape Town offices of Embrace Dignity, an organisation she set up in 2011. As well as offering support services for women exploited through prostitution, the group is lobbying for a change in the law that would mark a historic shift in the way South Africa deals with the sex trade. Right now, a person paid to have sex is criminalised, along with the man paying to sexually access her body. But Embrace Dignity want the state to recognise that in this scenario there is one offender, not two. Prostitution, Madlala-Routledge explains, is 'violence against women'. South Africa should have a law which 'does not revictimise the victims, a law that understands the power inequality between the buyer and the seller'. That law has come to be known internationally as the Sex Buyer Law or Nordic model. It makes paying for sex a criminal offence, but decriminalises selling sex, and provides support and exiting services for people involved in the trade; a three-pronged approach which recognises prostitution is a form of sexual exploitation. Its objective is to stem the demand that drives the sex trade. It has been adopted by three of the four countries ranked highest for gender equality worldwide: Sweden, Iceland and Norway.[1] Madlala-Routledge's work is now dedicated to ensuring South Africa joins them.

Born in South Africa in 1952, Madlala-Routledge has dedicated most of her adult life to working for social justice. While at university she joined an anti-apartheid group lead by fellow student Steve Biko, who would go on to be an iconic figure in the struggle and was murdered, aged thirty, in police custody. Madlala-Routledge's post-university path led to her joining the ANC underground movement. 'I was given the task specifically of organising women and that is when my consciousness about gender oppression was born, my understanding of the way which as a black woman, as a woman, I was treated differently'. She would go on to be a delegate at the Convention for a Democratic South Africa (CODESA I and II), the historic negotiations through which apartheid was ended. And on 27 April 1994, Nozizwe Madlala-Routledge was elected to parliament in South Africa's first democratic election.

On deciding to leave parliament fifteen years later, Madlala-Routledge had no intention of retiring from activism. It was 2009: South Africa was gearing up to host the FIFA World Cup, and there were growing public calls to respond to the imminent arrival of hundreds of thousands of football fans by decriminalising the entire prostitution trade; not just the act of being paid for sex (which Madlala-Routledge agreed should be decriminalised), but also paying for sex, pimping, brothel-keeping, the lot. 'There was a push basically coming from the industry in different forms for South Africa to open up this very lucrative industry.' So she started to mobilise resistance. '[We] drew up a statement and a petition, calling on the government of South Africa not to turn South Africa into a large pimp state.'

A striking feature of the drive to grant a World Cup-long amnesty for pimps and brothel keepers was the claim that this was actually in women's best interests; both women involved in prostitution and women who were not. The fact that full-scale impunity would enable procurers to extract maximum profit with minimum risk, while would-be punters could buy sexual access to women with zero prospect of being held accountable, was not the issue. No. The point was it would make *women* safer.

According to one South African MP, fully legalising prostitution ahead of the World Cup would be 'one of the things that would make it [the tournament] a success because we hear of many rapes, because people don't have access to them, women',[2] not to mention that it 'would bring us tax and would improve the lives of those who are not working'. A group called Sex Workers Education and Advocacy Task Force (SWEAT) welcomed the proposals, saying 'We would support any legalisation of sex work'.[3] Their reason for backing full legalisation of the trade was, according to SWEAT's director, Eric Harper, that people in prostitution 'would have access to labour law. They would have a contract. They would have sick leave, set working hours.'[4]

While in South Africa I visited Table Mountain with

Grizelda Grootboom, a campaigner with Embrace Dignity, and from the top we looked down over the streets of Cape Town where she had grown up. Grizelda told me she had first been paid for sex acts during her time living on the streets, having run away from home after being gang raped at the age of nine. I asked Grizelda what she thought about claims that prostitution is 'work' – the kind of activity you can draw up a list of health and safety regulations for. 'If it's such a work,' she asked incredulously, 'who's going to skill me to give a client a blow-job? Who's going to train me to do that, if I may ask? And how are you going to train me 'cause as far as I'm concerned a blow-job does not even go as far as keep it to this level. No, it goes as violent and roughly, you cannot even breathe, your eyes are watering, it's halfway down your throat, you feel like puking and the person is holding your head, their hand on your hair and pulling you back and forth. So who's going to train me to do that?'

Given that 'prostitution itself is a form of violence against women', as Madlala-Routledge said, the idea that you could apply health and safety regulations to its enactment – that you could make sexual abuse 'safe' – is plainly nonsensical. And the idea that government should sanction it, tax it, issue licences to the venues where it takes place, flies in the face of the notion of equal citizenship.

'While we have the demand for prostitution not being addressed we cannot achieve gender equality,' insists Madlala-Routledge. 'Men who buy sex don't regard the woman as a whole human being. Basically they regard her as an object

– something that's available to them for their satisfaction for the money . . . So basically that says to us this can't be somebody you treat as an equal, this can't be somebody you treat as having dignity, as being a whole human being, for you to actually treat them like that or think of them like that.' I asked Madlala-Routledge about this notion of dignity, about why she chose to include it in the name of her organisation. 'Apartheid itself was a form of not recognising the dignity of black people. The experience of being treated as an underdog was very present as we wrote our constitution, and we wanted South Africa to be a different place.' The constitution of South Africa is familiar to Madlala-Routledge not just because she frequently refers to it in her work, but because she helped write it. As well as participating in the CODESA negotiations, Madlala-Routledge was part of the Women's National Coalition which 'adopted the charter for effective gender equality, and a lot of the rights in that charter I included in our constitution. We fought for that.' So Madlala-Routledge is not about to sit back and watch that foundational principle of equality abandoned in practice. 'We wanted for everyone in South Africa to enjoy human dignity. So that came up really at the top of the rights that we felt had been trampled for many years and therefore we prize it very, very highly. And what Embrace Dignity is doing is saying, but you can't prize it only for men. This is a right that women as full human beings with equal rights need to also enjoy.'

In the end, the opposition was strong enough to stop the sex trade being legalised in South Africa. However, calls to implement this proposal on a permanent basis persist. And not just in South Africa. The fantastical notion that the interests of pimps, punters and women (both inside and outside the trade) happen to perfectly legally align now underpins a serious and sustained global push for countries to make all aspects of prostitution legal. At the core of this bid is the wholesale denial of the sexual abuse and objectification inherent to the sex trade, the sexist roots of its demand, and its dire implications for the status of women and girls. Total legalisation (or full 'decriminalisation') is the myth of prostitution as 'sex work' made into law.

Violence against women is something that states should work to end: it's not a complicated notion. Lest any legislature be confused or indifferent on the matter, there is a raft of international laws requiring it. Chief among them: the Convention for the Elimination of All Forms of Discrimination Against Women (CEDAW), otherwise known as the women's bill of rights, which 189 states are a party to.[5] When it comes to prostitution, as with any form of violence against women, there is no 'neutral' position for a state to take on the matter. The prostitution trade currently exists but, as I've argued, it is not inevitable. The current desire and willingness of some men to pay for sexual access to another person's body is manufactured by unequal power relations between women and men. So the state has a choice: it can pursue, or not pursue, policies to grow, contain, shrink or end the sex trade.

The choice about whether to grow, contain, shrink or end commercial sexual exploitation really shouldn't be a difficult one. Violence against women: bad (even the profitable kinds); ergo, work to end it. Legal frameworks that make paying for sex, pimping and brothel-keeping legal are not designed to end the prostitution trade, of course. Pimping women on the street, running brothel networks; these aren't teenage-style rebellions that the exploiters will promptly ditch if the state decides to get down with it and sanction their profiteering. To promote total legalisation of the sex trade is to deny that working to end prostitution is an option, or, at least, a desirable option. And why would it be desirable if you maintain that it's actually just a form of regular work?

In 2008 the parents of Marnie Frey, a young woman murdered by Canadian serial killer Robert Pickton, published an open letter after learning of calls to legalise prostitution. Rick and Lynn Frey wrote,

> Our daughter was forced into prostitution because of the need to feed her addiction to drugs. To think of prostitution as a 'job' and treat it as such is ridiculous. I am disgusted to think that anyone would think that prostitution is a job. It is not. It is violence against women. Neither legalizing prostitution nor having a brothel would have prevented the murder of our daughter . . . To think the best we can do for these women is giving them a safe place to sell their bodies is a joke. There is no such thing as a 'clean safe place' to be abused in.[6]

And yet, some states have attempted to create exactly that.

Legalisation laboratories

'Prostitution has existed for a long time and will continue to do so,'[7] insisted the Netherlands' minister of justice in 1999. The country's decision to lift the ban on brothels and pimping and regulate the trade instead, beginning the following year, would allow it to 'become healthy, safe, transparent and cleansed from criminal side-effects'.[8] Similarly, a report by the German federal government explains that the country's decision to legalise the trade, enacted on 1 January 2002, was based on the belief that the 'risks and dangers' associated with prostitution were 'primarily determined by the conditions under which the prostitutes are working'.[9] Prostitution was 'taken as a given';[10] the objective was to enable people that men paid to perform sex acts on them to 'conclude proper employment contracts' and to 'improve the prostitutes' health and hygiene conditions at work.' The messaging of 'health and safety' was yet again mobilised when New Zealand 'decriminalised' the prostitution trade the following year. The purpose of the new law, its official evaluators tell us, was 'to neither decrease, nor increase, the number of people involved in the sex industry; but to provide sex workers the same protections enjoyed by other workers in New Zealand.'[11]

A quick note on terminology: New Zealand's prostitution law is usually labelled as 'decriminalisation', rather than 'legalisation'. The difference, it's argued, is that in a decriminalised regime there are no criminal laws specifically curtailing prostitution or connected activities like pimping and brothel-keeping. In a legalised prostitution regime, such as in Germany and the Netherlands, states impose 'restrictions on how, when and where sex work happens',[12] as the NSWP put it, like banning prostitution in certain areas or imposing operating rules on brothels. And yet, New Zealand's prostitution regime doesn't actually meet the conditions of 'decriminalisation'. The 2003 Prostitution Reform Act, which scraped through New Zealand's parliament by a single vote, allows territorial authorities to restrict prostitution advertising and the location of brothels, and it bans people on a temporary entry class visa from selling sex or running or investing in a brothel. On top of that, a person in prostitution is actually breaking the law if she fails to adopt 'safer sex practices' and faces a potential fine of $2000.[13] So women paid for sex can still be criminalised in this so-called decriminalised regime.

Confused application of terms aside, it's difficult to decide which in principle – full decriminalisation or legalisation – is worse. Total market liberation, where the laissez-faire state sits back and lets brothel owners have free reign over 'how, when and where' to ply their profitable exploits, or a slightly more interventionist approach, where the legitimating state peers over pimps' shoulders to make sure they're doing it 'right'. Either way, these are state responses to male violence against women which do not seek to end the violence – because they don't recognise the inherent sexual abuse, or because they deem it inevitable.

But not only do these approaches fail to address (or acknowledge) the inherent harm of prostitution, they fail even on their own terms of preventing the trade's 'attendant' harms – like pimping, trafficking and coercion by brothel keepers. As I will show, on multiple counts, full legalisation or so-called decriminalisation simply magnifies these harms. The contradictions and casualties wrought by these testing grounds reveal the mythical nature of claims that the sex trade can be treated as a form of work, which decriminalisation will make 'safe'.

Pimps

When the Dutch government legalised prostitution in 2000 it lifted the country's ban on pimping.[14] It was claimed that by stepping in and regulating prostitution as a legitimate trade, it would be possible 'to reorganise the prostitution sector and purge it of criminal peripheral phenomena, and to combat the exploitation of people [in] prostitution (in the form of involuntary prostitution or prostitution by minors) more forcefully'.[15] Germany legalised pimping the following year, scrapping penalties for the 'promotion of prostitution',[16] while introducing a new crime of 'exploitation of prostitutes'.* Now there was a wrong way to pimp, and a right way to pimp. (The wrong way could, for example, involve a pimp taking more than fifty per cent of a person's prostitution earnings.[17]) Germany's rationale for dropping pimping penalties was similar to the Netherlands'. Because the state would be

* In Germany there were 151 convictions for procurement in 2000, prior to the legalisation of prostitution. In 2011, there were just thirty-two.[18]

regulating the trade and allowing brothels to issue employment contracts, it was assumed, a government evaluation later explained, that this would 'reduce [women's] dependency
on, for example, pimps and to improve the prostitutes' health
and hygiene conditions at work.'[19] So there would be no need
for a flat-out ban on pimping.

Turns out, lifting prohibitions on pimping does not, in
fact, precipitate a downpour of feminist fairy dust, causing
pimping to disappear or magically transform into a non-ex-
ploitative practice. Nor, it would seem, does legalising pimping mean that when procurers do it 'wrong' (e.g. they exert
'too much' control or the 'wrong kind' of control) the words
pimp-controlled appear written across a woman's forehead,
clear as day for police and passers-by to see. An evaluation of
the Netherlands' legalised prostitution regime seven years after
the law was adopted, commissioned for the Dutch parliament,
found that pimping was 'still a very common phenomenon'[20]
and 'does not seem to have decreased'. Fieldwork researchers
reported that the 'great majority'[21] of women in window brothels, for which Amsterdam is famed, work 'with a so-called
boyfriend or pimp'. Window brothels, along with escorting
and home-based prostitution, were deemed most conducive
to the pimps' task of monitoring women. The reality, the evaluation concluded, was that 'some preconditions required for
a [brothel] licence are easy to check, but to actually observe
exploitation of people or coercion is extremely difficult'.[22]

Even when it comes to issuing a brothel licence, researchers at VU University Amsterdam note the 'common problem'

of 'straw men' being used to front brothels, allowing other (non-licensed) sex trade profiteers to retain control behind the scenes.[23] They highlight a police investigation that found 'direct negotiations about rooms took place with pimps (rather than prostitutes) and that a cafe was used as a meeting place for pimps, where they could monitor their prostitutes in the alley via the cafe's surveillance cameras'. In 2014 a large brothel business in Amsterdam's red light district had its application to renew its licence turned down on the basis that at least three victims of sex trafficking had been exploited in the company's window brothels, with police reportedly finding an additional twenty women who may have been forced to be there.[24]

What makes pimping impervious to government decrees that prostitution is merely 'work' is that the apt comparison for the relationship concerned is not that of agent and client, but domestic violence. Sometimes, it's one and the same. A study into the experiences of 100 women in Chicago controlled by a pimp found 64 women described their pimp as their boyfriend or 'man'.[25] Coercive control – a pattern of manipulation at the core of domestic violence – played a pivotal role in the relationship, including at 'recruitment stage', with over half of the women disclosing that this form of abuse was used to encourage them into prostitution. A range of controlling tactics were employed by pimps, who 'verbally abused 85 per cent of the women, threatened to end a romantic relationship with 69 per cent, took money from 69 per cent, and threatened harm to 68 per cent. In addition,

63 per cent of the women reported being indebted to their pimps because of the provision of food, clothing, and gifts.' Additionally, 75 per cent of women confirmed that their pimp subjected them to violence.

The striking commonalities between the behaviour of pimps and domestic violence perpetrators were also found by researchers to be in evidence in Amsterdam's legal, licensed window brothels. Analysing twelve police investigations into trafficking in this sector and involving a total of 76 victims, it became clear that women were often locked into an 'intimate relationship' with their exploiters.[26] The relationship would commonly start out seeming positive. 'X listened to me when I talked about my feelings and I felt he was someone I could talk to really well,' one woman recalled. But then the control, the isolation, the violence would creep in. 'We always had to report if we went somewhere, we could not go out with men, we had to describe in detail who we spoke to, or who smiled at us.' Escape routes were psychologically and physically cut off. One woman recounted telling her 'boyfriend' she wanted to leave: 'He then smacked me. Like this! Three blows to my head with his fists. Things went black before my eyes three times. I started to cry. Then he said, "Embrace me, embrace me, embrace me now." I just did what I was told. Ever since I've never gathered the courage to say that I wanted to leave him.' The study's authors also relay an attempt to escape by one woman exploited in an Amsterdam window brothel: 'She closed the curtain as if she had a customer and called a cab. The taxi stopped in front of the building and she got in.

However, the taxi was intercepted by one of the trafficker's "bodyguards".' The woman was taken back to her exploiter.

Pimping is commercial sexual exploitation. Making it legal does not miraculously deter would-be exploiters, nor support those they subject to coercive control to get away.

Trafficking

Germany legalised prostitution, the government's 2007 evaluation of the law explains, on the basis that 'it must be possible to limit the problematical aspects associated with it by taking prostitution out of the shadows'.[27] One of those 'problematical aspects' is, of course, sex trafficking. Six years after the Bundestag legalised brothels and pimping, the federal government's review conceded that there was 'no firm evidence' its objective of taking the trade out of 'the shadows' had been achieved.[28] Helmut Sporer, of the Crimes Squad in the German city of Augsburg, leads local efforts to combat sex trafficking. He has worked in this area for around twenty years, witnessing firsthand the consequences of legalisation. The effect has been so dramatic that he publicly declared Germany, with its legalised prostitution regime, 'the El Dorado for pimps'.[29] He reported, 'The liberal regulations have led to the emergence of a complete industry in the trafficking of women, with both small and large retailers delivering women to the brothels.'

In 2013 local officials banned street prostitution in Augsburg (which the federal law allows them to do) because pimping and trafficking, particularly of women from Hungary, Romania and Bulgaria, had become such an overwhelming problem in the street 'scene'. Today Sporer estimates that around ninety per cent of women in Augsburg's prostitution trade come from abroad, mostly from south-east Europe. I asked Sporer what practical impact legalising brothels and pimping has had on his ability to combat trafficking. 'At the moment there are increasing numbers of brothels,' he said, and the reality is, 'monitoring prostitution [is] very difficult. Many women are not registered anywhere; they are effectively outside the system.' So the scale of the problem has been magnified.

It is also extremely difficult to convict brothel operators connected to trafficking networks because, usually, 'personal evidence is necessary to ensure a conviction. That means that victims have to give evidence against the suspects in court. Many victims won't speak out because for fear of reprisals. Over and over again one hears of cases where victims' dependants living in their home countries face intimidation.' Sporer's team do manage to secure convictions on occasion though. He recounted one such case at a meeting held by the European Women's Lobby in 2013:

[This] Hungarian trafficker [was] a really large 'retailer' . . . He had acted as an agent for several brothels in Germany and Austria and placed up to 150 women there per year. The brothels ordered the women from him as in a catalogue, sorted according to size, hair colour, figure etc. And this major retailer even offered a return of merchandise guarantee, if the woman didn't please or did not meet the demands of the customer.[30]

Eight years after brothels and pimping were legalised in the Netherlands, the national police force estimated that between fifty and ninety per cent of women paid for sex in the country's legal prostitution trade 'work involuntarily'.[31] This study was prompted by the Sneep Case, then the biggest trafficking case ever taken to trial in the Netherlands. Five men were convicted of participating in an extensive trafficking network. The court judgement recorded that it was 'characterised by its ruthless and violent practices'.[32] Over 100 women are thought to have been sexually exploited by these men. And it all took place through the Netherlands' visible, legal, licensed brothels.[33]

In 2008, Amsterdam's mayor, Job Cohen, was reported in the *New York Times* declaring that that the Dutch attempt to introduce 'transparency' through legalisation had failed. 'We realize that this hasn't worked, that trafficking in women continues,'[34] he said. 'You can't normalize this business.' Similarly, researchers at VU University Amsterdam, who analysed trafficking in a legalised prostitution market, concluded in 2014: 'the screening of brothel owners and the monitoring of the compliance of licensing conditions do not create levels of transparency that enable sex trafficking to be exposed'.[35] In fact, their assessment suggests it can make exposing it harder. 'The regulation has hidden the legalized sector from the view of the criminal justice system, while human trafficking still thrives behind the legal façade of a legalized prostitution sector. Brothels can even function as legalized outlets for victims of sex trafficking.'

The influential role of prostitution laws on trafficking dynamics is also evident at an international level. Trafficking flows are larger into countries where prostitution is legal; that was the conclusion of a cross-sectional analysis of up to 150 countries.[36] A separate study restricted to European countries also found sex trafficking to be most prevalent in nations with legalised prostitution regimes.[37] It was least prevalent where prostitution was completely illegal, and 'in between' in countries where buying and selling sex were legal but pimping and brothel-keeping weren't. The researchers suggest 'slacker prostitution laws make it more profitable to traffick persons to a country'.

Violence

According to billionaire financier George Soros's philanthropic organisation, the Open Society Foundations, fully decriminalising the prostitution trade means that people paid to have sex are more likely to live free from the fear of violence.[38] Its publication, 'Ten reasons to decriminalize sex work', declares: 'When sex work is decriminalized, sex workers are empowered to realize their right to work safely, and to use the justice system to seek redress for abuses and discrimination.'[39] The report repeatedly cites New Zealand's decriminalised prostitution regime as an exemplar. Under

Reason 4, 'Decriminalization promotes safe working conditions', the Open Society Foundations tells us that 'Decriminalization in New Zealand brought sex workers under the Health and Safety in Employment Act, resulting in the creation of occupational health guidelines, which sex workers have used to assert their rights with employers and clients.'

The occupational health and safety guidelines the Open Society Foundations refer to include top tips for brothel owners, like 'Install safety devices such as accessible alarm buttons in all rooms' and 'Acknowledge and maintain the right of sex workers to refuse any client'.[40] Although, in a section on 'Personal Protective Equipment', under the heading 'Condom breakage or slippage', the guidelines note, 'Unfortunately, incidents occur where workers are forced by clients to have sex without a condom against their will (i.e. rape). Sex without a condom can result where the client removes or breaks the condom during the service without the worker's knowledge. In these situations, the employee must have information and support on taking appropriate action (see Fact Sheet 3).' (Another reason given to check out Fact Sheet 3 – 'Action to be taken in the event of condom breakage or slippage' – is that 'Unintended pregnancy may be a consequence of working in the sex industry.')

As evidence of their proclamations that fully decriminalising the sex trade promotes women's safety, the Open Society Foundations cite a review of the law commissioned by the New Zealand government, published five years after it was adopted. Aside from neglecting to mention that the review itself acknowledged that compliance with the Health and Safety in Employment Act 'cannot be measured as there is no system of regular inspections of brothels',[41] the Open Society Foundations report's uniformly positive references to New Zealand's law review does rather beg the question of whether the authors had actually read it.

A survey of 772 women in prostitution conducted for New Zealand's official law review found that, in the previous 12 months, 42 per cent of women who sold sex on the street and 38 per cent of those who sold sex in 'managed indoor' venues 'felt they had to accept a client when they didn't want to'.[42]* The review states, 'The overall impression gained by the [Crime and Justice Research Centre] in their interviews was that there were "good" and "bad" [brothel] operators as regards allowing sex workers to refuse to provide commercial sexual services. The good ones tended to accept a worker's judgement, but even so insisted on their having a "good" reason to refuse.'[44] Also in the last 12 months, 13 per cent of women selling sex on the street and 10 per cent in managed brothels revealed that a sex buyer had physically assaulted them, while 3 per cent and 5 per cent selling sex in managed brothels and on the street respectively disclosed they had been raped by a sex buyer. Interviews with women revealed 'the majority felt that the [Prostitution Reform Act] could do little about the violence that occurred'

---

* The review says that when it came to conducting the survey of women's experiences in the prostitution trade, 'Participants whose English was not sufficient to understand the questions without the aid of an interpreter were excluded.'[43]

and 'few' of the women had reported any of the violence to which they had been subjected to the police. Also in the official review of New Zealand's prostitution law, a brothel operator is quoted as saying, '[Brothel lisences] are too easy to get. I've lost confidence in the system. I used to be a car dealer and to get a licence was really hard. For this, there is no training, no interview, no asking what you know. What's the point?'[45]

Perhaps the enthusiasm of some pro-decriminalisation lobby groups to use New Zealand as a touchstone reference can be partly accounted for by the inexplicably sunny outlook and minimal recommendations for reform put forward by the Prostitution Law Review Committee, which authored the official review. Because despite the ongoing rates of violence, despite the evaluators being 'very concerned' that there were evidently brothels requiring women to 'provide commercial sexual services against their will', despite even brothel keepers declaring the licensing regime lax to the point of pointless, the Committee concluded the following: 'regulation should initially be kept to a minimum'[46] and 'applicants should not be required to pass a test on their rights and responsibilities as brothel operators before being supplied with an operator's certificate. Rather, they should be provided with information about these matters at the time of receipt of a certificate.' (Oh, and the Committee felt that requiring brothel operators to review their certificates on an annual basis was 'unnecessarily frequent'. The law, they said, should be changed so that brothel owners need only reapply every three years.)

Looking over the Prostitution Law Review Committee's

recommendations, researchers at London Metropolitan University's Child and Woman Abuse Studies Unit (CWASU) dubbed the report 'surprisingly complacent'.[47] Personally, I didn't find the complacency particularly surprising after looking at who was on the eleven-strong committee. It included three people officially nominated by a group that played a leading role in securing the law in the first place,* as well as a woman nominated by the minister of commerce whose relevant qualifications, the committee's report tells us, were that she had 'developed and written a user friendly job description and interview booklet for sex workers' and that 'for the past ten years Ms Brennan has managed brothels'.[48]

'Working conditions'

Legalised prostitution regimes embody the fundamentally abhorrent notion of attempting to create a 'clean safe place' for paying punters to commit sexual abuse in. On top of that, the failed attempts by states to apply 'safety measures' to prostitution from the world of regular work – like employment contracts and health and safety rules – betray legislative endeavours that were either 'reprehensibly naive',[49] as an Amsterdam alderman (now the deputy prime minister) dubbed his country's decision in 2011, or just not particularly serious about their stated aims.

---

* It is written into the Prostitution Reform Act itself that the Prostitution Law Review Committee must include '3 persons nominated by the New Zealand Prostitutes Collective'.[50]

When the German Bundestag legalised the prostitution trade, one of its key objectives was 'to enable the prostitutes to conclude proper employment contracts'.[51] Legalising brothels, the rationale went, would boost women's safety by opening up legal rights afforded to any employee of a business vis-à-vis their working conditions, and employment contracts were the key to those rights. Except, it turned out, most women in prostitution didn't actually want a contract, and brothel keepers, unsurprisingly, didn't want to issue them. For brothel owners, the prospect of shouldering the responsibility and costs as an employer, while being restricted in their ability to issue orders to employees (if a woman didn't want to 'serve' a sex buyer, legally, she didn't have to), was not, apparently, an attractive one. Interviews with women in prostitution conducted for the Government's 2007 evaluation revealed that just 1 per cent had an employment contract and only 6 per cent wanted one.[52] Reasons women gave for not wanting a contract included concerns over the powers it would grant brothel owners over them, fears it would compromise their anonymity, and not wishing to stay in the prostitution trade – seeing their involvement as temporary. 'Hardly any' women paid for sex had registered with a social insurance agency, with some insurers unwilling to offer insurance 'on account of the negative risk assessment associated with working as a prostitute'.

It was much the same story when New Zealand reviewed its prostitution regime. The 'standard position' was that women in brothels were self-employed[53] (though, in principle, rules could still be imposed on brothels via the licensing regime). And in the Netherlands, where the official evaluation found that brothel owners and women who sell sex 'stubbornly maintain'[54] that the latter are self-employed and that 'labour relations in the licensed businesses have scarcely changed; there has been no significant improvement.' The implications of brothels not issuing contracts, and most women not wanting them, is that women paid for sex are not only denied certain entitlements, they are laden with legal obligations. As New Zealand's Prostitution Law Review Committee pointed out, by virtue of being 'independent contractors' in brothels, women there are denied basic guarantees like sick pay, and they themselves have responsibilities under health and safety law which, if not fulfilled, can result in 'serious financial consequences' for them.[55]

How about robust, ongoing monitoring of brothels, then? One might presume this would be indispensable if brothels are to comply with certain rules. (New Zealand's 'health and safety guide for the sex trade', for example, sets out 'general requirements for cleanliness, providing fire extinguishers, or repairing faulty electrical equipment',[56] as well as identifying what it calls 'hazards in the workplace' – like the risk of sexually transmitted infections or unwanted pregnancy.) Well, when Germany legalised prostitution it didn't even require brothels to apply for a licence before opening,[57] let alone impose a rigorous regulatory scheme. Nor did the Prostitution Act contain any 'positive regulations'[58] regarding conditions in the newly legalised brothels. A study commissioned for the federal government's review of the law quotes a trade licensing officer saying, 'With brothels [we] are dealing with a highly criminal milieu and yet we allow ourselves as the state to scrutinize them less than we do a restaurateur who runs an eight-star restaurant. This contradiction alone makes the situation untenable for me. We are deluding ourselves here, because we simply don't want to deal with these things.'[59] Because so few women in prostitution have an employment contract, the federal government's review also notes that as a consequence, 'existing mechanisms for monitoring working conditions, such as state and professional association health and safety laws, are largely not applied in prostitution'.[60]

New Zealand did impose a licensing scheme for brothels – but only those with more than four people selling sex from them. As already mentioned though, there was no ongoing inspection system to accompany it. One of the consequences of this monitoring vacuum is alluded to by the Prostitution Law Review Committee: 'Police also reported that investigation into suspected employment of *underage workers* in brothels or small owner-operated brothels has been more limited since the enactment of the PRA [Prostitution Reform Act 2003]. This is because: police now have no right of entry into brothels or other premises; brothel owners are not required to maintain a record of the age identification of sex workers or provide it to police.'[61] (Italics mine; and the committee didn't actually recommend altering either of these conditions.)

For a prostitution regime frequently held up as proof of the health-and-safety-boosting properties of full decriminalisation, New Zealand's own review is damning. It states:

'Generally, brothels which had treated their workers fairly prior to the enactment of the PRA continued to do so, and those which had unfair management practices continued with them.'

'The CJRC's [Crime and Justice Research Centre] key informants were not aware of any substantial change in the use of safer sex practices by sex workers as a result of the enactment of the PRA.'

'Although it was hoped decriminalisation would make it easier for sex workers to access health services, the CSOM [Christchurch School of Medicine] study found that there were no significant differences in access to health services between Christchurch participants in 1999 and 2006.'

'The Committee considers that the purpose of the PRA, particularly in terms of promoting the welfare and occupational health and safety of sex workers, cannot be fully realised in the street-based sector.'[62]

For Sarah O'Brien, an employment lawyer based in New Zealand, the idea that her country's prostitution regime offers credibility to the positive claims made of decriminalisation simply doesn't stand up. 'If the New Zealand model is being used as a template for making women safer, it doesn't work. It hasn't worked. It has not had that effect,' she told me. 'It set out to minimise the harm to women in prostitution and it hasn't done that. And there's no argument that it hasn't done that. What it has done is push through the agenda of the sex industry owners and I suspect that that was the real agenda to start with. It's made things very easy for them and it's made things very easy for sex buyers.'

I met Sarah in 2015 in England ahead of a speech she was giving at the Oxford Union later that same day. The university debating society was deliberating the motion, 'This house embraces sex work as a career choice'. Sarah was there to report on what happens when a state parliament effectively votes 'yes' to this.

There are repeated references in the Prostitution Law Review Committee's report to the issue of stigma, and its potential role in hindering efforts to boost 'working conditions'. The review concludes that 'Despite decriminalisation, the social stigma surrounding involvement in the sex industry continues.'[63] But Sarah is scathing when I ask her about attempts to frame this as the main reason harms in prostitution so evidently persist, and the claim that making brothel-keeping and pimping legal helps matters:

> I really think it's a ridiculous argument. If you look at Germany with its legalisation model, if you look at New Zealand with its decriminalised model, if you look at Victoria in Australia, these are jurisdictions that have tried this for a long time now. You would think if this is the way forward – to make prostitution a job like any other and eliminate stigma – then it would be gone.

But that's not what's happening in New Zealand, Sarah says.

> I just don't see there being any reduction in the general
> community's attitude towards prostitution as a result of
> this act. What I do see is an increasing callousness in male
> attitudes towards women in our country . . . The attitude
> that [paying for sex] is acceptable and normal behaviour
> – normalisation of this – which [is] what's happening in
> New Zealand. Boys are being brought up thinking that
> this is fine. It's legal, why is it a problem?

The wider attitudes fuelled by legally enshrining prostitution
as work are not ones that make women safer, Sarah insists.
'You just get this end result of a real callous disregard for
young girls and women. And I think this is going to be the
legacy of the Prostitution Reform Act.'

Entry and exit

Appeals to the mythical health-and-safety-boosting potential
of legalising pimping and brothel-keeping tend to fix on the
present, on people currently involved in the trade. But what
about the before and after? What impact does categorising
prostitution as work in law have on routes into prostitution,
and the possibility of a route out?

During New Zealand's 2008 review of its prostitution regime, approximately 770 people who sold sex were asked why
they became involved. A quarter said that one of their reasons

for entering prostitution was that the trade was 'no longer illegal'.[64] (The Prostitution Law Review Committee was quick to cast doubt on the relevance of their own finding, however, stating 'Workers who had considered the legal status of sex work were not asked whether they would have entered the sex industry if it was still illegal. Therefore, it is not possible to know whether decriminalisation precipitated their entry, or whether they would have started sex work regardless'.)

The fact that Germany's prostitution trade was state-sanctioned was certainly a critical factor in Marie's decision to enter it. 'If it hadn't been legal I wouldn't have done it,' she explained to me at her home in Germany. 'My situation was complicated enough. So I wouldn't, you know, as I wouldn't rob an old lady or as I won't steal at the shop or something like that. I wouldn't have made this decision if it wouldn't have been so easy and legal. I really had wished that it wasn't legal and the state – we say "father state" in Germany, you know we call the state "the father" – and I really had the wish that the father had protected me from that with a good law.'

There is also clear evidence that legal frameworks affect the overall size of prostitution markets. In their analysis of prostitution regimes in nine countries, researchers at CWASU observed that 'legalised and unregulated regimes have considerably larger sex industries'.[65] Dr Maddy Coy and her colleagues at CWASU also concluded from their research on men who pay for sex that 'legality contributes to normalisation, which in turn increases the likelihood of paying for sex'.[66]

It is worth noting that in its report of New Zealand's so-called decriminalised regime, the Prostitution Law Review Committee felt able to conclude that decriminalisation 'has had little impact'[67] on the number of women paid for sex. But they included this caveat: 'The Committee wishes to emphasise the difficulty of accurately assessing the number of people involved in the sex industry, even in the current decriminalised environment.' Indeed, there certainly wasn't uniform agreement about the relative size of the trade. Streetreach, an organisation delivering support to people involved in street prostitution, reported that there had been an increase in the Auckland region since the law changed, with an 'influx of sex workers on the streets in the six to eight months prior to June 2007'. However, CWASU notes that historically New Zealand has not had an especially large sex trade, 'and this, coupled with its small dispersed population* and geographic isolation has meant it is one of very few countries not to have had a considerable increase in trafficking for sexual exploitation over the past decade'.[68] Indeed, the Prostitution Law Review Committee acknowledged the country's relative appeal to traffickers is mediated by its 'geographical isolation'.[69]

Once involved in prostitution, the practical and psychological barriers to getting out can be immense. Mia de Faoite explained to me that she had gone into prostitution just intending to tide herself and her girlfriend over for a while.

---

* New Zealand's population as of 2015 was approximately 4.6 million. [70]

They both had a drug addiction, and the money had run out. 'You never think a few months will turn into the five years or whatever. But I knew I had done some serious damage to my mind.' Mia was raped on three separate occasions while in prostitution:

> I just carried on 'cause I knew heroin was my support system and I thought if it was gone I would just crack up. And I couldn't. I was the only person in my daughter's life, really. And I just couldn't lose my mind. You're caught in this paradox and it's quite a strange place to be . . . You go in there to pay for a drug you're addicted to. But you end up taking more of that drug to cope with being in the place you went to go to fix the heroin.

The prospect of getting out seemed a long way from her day-to-day reality. 'Nobody had a gun to our head. The chains are not visible,' she explained. 'In there it's lonely and it's isolating and it keeps you there longer because you don't understand the outside world anymore.'

The provision of specialist support services can prove critical to whether women are able to exit the sex trade. Yet if a government fails to recognise pimping, brothel-keeping and sex buying as sexual exploitation, if instead it chooses to regularise these activities, manage them, levy taxes on them, it begs the question of why the government would then set up parallel mechanisms to support women to get out. If the message from the top is prostitution is work, not abuse, why have an exiting system?

It's a question that hangs over official evaluations of legalised prostitution regimes such as in Germany and the Netherlands. The German federal government's 2007 assessment
remarked on the 'rather sobering picture'[71] painted by its investigations into the availability of exiting services. 'The Prostitution Act has not recognisably improved the prostitutes'
means for leaving prostitution,' it concluded. The Netherlands devolved decisions on precisely how to regulate the
legalised prostitution trade to local municipalities. When it
came to collecting country-wide data for the national parliament, published in 2007, it was found that just 6 per cent of
municipalities addressed 'the possibilities to leave the prostitution business'[72] in their local prostitution policy.

New Zealand's Prostitution Law Reform Committee, for
its part, noted that when it comes to supporting people to
exit prostitution, 'adequate resourcing is vital to ensure good
service provision'.[73] They conceded, however, that 'the very
fact of decriminalisation may make funding harder to get.'
The committee cited previous research into prostitution regimes which concluded this: 'It would seem that once prostitution is legalised governments want to pretend the problem
has gone away.' To ascertain how well their own country had
fared in carving out exit routes for people involved in prostitution, the committee asked New Zealand's eighty-four local authorities 'whether they had done anything to assist sex
workers to exit the industry.' Just two said yes. Most said it
was central government's job. So the committee asked the
relevant central government agencies what support they

offered. None operated programmes targeted at women in prostitution.

The notion that making pimping and brothel-keeping legal makes women safe is not only mythical, it's farcical. And yet, full decriminalisation of prostitution is now advocated by some of the world's most prestigious intergovernmental and humanitarian institutions. In 2012 the WHO, UNFPA and UNAIDS joined together to put out a report advising countries to 'work toward decriminalization of sex work'[74] in order to tackle HIV and other sexually transmitted infections. And in 2015, the leadership of Amnesty International passed a policy endorsing full decriminalisation of the sex trade – brothel-keeping and pimping included – 'to protect the human rights of sex workers'.[75]

How could the incredible notion that women's safety would be boosted by enshrining prostitution in the statute books as 'work', while re-categorising brothel keepers as legitimate business owners, become as credible as it has on the international stage?

Full decriminalisation gains some powerful champions

The story of how the call to legalise brothel-keeping and pimping came to be amplified through the global megaphone of UN agencies is one of catastrophic failings to identify and address violence against women; an ignominious part of history when humanitarian institutions wound up advocating for a 'clean safe place' for women to be abused in. It is the story of the myth that total decriminalisation of the sex trade would make women safer being swallowed hook, line and sinker. And to start to understand how this could have happened, you have to know who Alejandra Gil is.

On 12 Thursday March 2015, sixty-four-year-old Alejandra Gil was convicted in Mexico City of sex trafficking and sentenced to fifteen years in prison. Gil controlled a pimping operation that exploited approximately 200 women, and was reported to be one of the most powerful pimps of Sullivan Street, an area of Mexico City notorious for prostitution.[76] Known as the 'Madam of Sullivan', Gil and her son were connected with trafficking networks in Tlaxcala state[77] – home to a city dubbed Mexico's 'epicenter for sex trafficking'.[78]

In addition to her daily pimping duties, Alejandra Gil had a sideline as president of Aproase, an NGO claiming to advocate for the rights of people in prostitution, but reportedly functioning as a useful cover for her pimping operation.[79] And until Gil's arrest on 14 February 2014, the 'Madam of Sullivan' was vice-president of the NSWP, an organisation already highlighted as being at the forefront of efforts to recognise brothel-keeping and pimping as legitimate work.

It's easy to see why someone like Alejandra Gil would have been invested in peddling the myth that making brothels and pimping legal makes women safer, and why she would spend years advocating for total decriminalisation in her role as vice-president of NSWP. What is not so easy to see, however, is how Gil could come to be personally acknowledged in the WHO's 2012 report advocating full decriminalisation as one of the 'experts' who dedicated her 'time and expertise' to developing its recommendations.[80] NSWP's logo is on the front cover, right alongside the logos of WHO, UNAIDS and UN-FPA. What is also astonishing is that NSWP were invited to co-chair a UNAIDS advisory group with an express mandate to 'review and participate in the development of UNAIDS policy, programme or advocacy documents, or statements'.[81] It is astonishing, because it really shouldn't take the conviction of one of its leaders for sex trafficking to work out who benefits most from the agenda to make brothel-keeping, pimping and, of course, sex buying, legal around the world.

2007 was a pivotal year in NSWP's quest to get their call for the decriminalisation of brothels and pimping taken seriously. UNAIDS published a guidance note on how to respond to the HIV crisis in the context of a prostitution trade. While using the euphemistic terminology of 'sex work', the report nonetheless observed that 'Male attitudes and behaviours, gender-based violence, sexual exploitation, and stigma and discrimination against women and girls continue to be critical contributing factors driving the HIV epidemic. These culturally and socially ascribed roles contribute to men's demand for paid sex.'[82] The UN agency concluded that in order to tackle the HIV crisis it was important to tackle demand for prostitution: 'the overwhelming majority of sex workers are women and, conversely, the overwhelming majority of their clients are men. While cultural constructs influence gender relations, leading to the demand for sex work, culture itself is not an immutable construct: it is possible and timely to achieve social change, and consequently behavioural change among men, to reduce the demand for sex work.'

Needless to say, this didn't go down well with Alejandra Gil's organisation. A working group established by NSWP wrote to the UNAIDS' executive director about their 'concern' with the report's 'emphasis on reducing commercial sex'.[83] The leadership of UNAIDS took the staggering decision to appoint this organisation, which expressly lobbies for pimping and brothel-keeping to be made legal, as co-chairs of a new 'UNAIDS Advisory Group on HIV and Sex Work'.[84] It is worth noting that NSWP didn't attempt to mask their objective of squashing efforts to end the prostitution trade. Minutes from the advisory group's first meeting note agreement that 'UNAIDS' focus and advice in the context of sex work should be reduction in the demand for unprotected sex',[85] as opposed to demand for prostitution. It records: 'Any emphasis on reduction of the demand for paid sex could result in important resources being diverted from HIV prevention to implementing policies that are ineffective or, *in the worst case*, criminalise and discourage clients purchasing sexual services.' (Italics mine.)

NSWP's lobbying efforts paid off. In 2009 a revised version of the UNAIDS guidance note was published. This time it carried an annex prepared by the agency's new advisory group. It duly recommends: 'States should move away from criminalising sex work or activities associated with it. Decriminalisation of sex work should include removing criminal laws and penalties for purchase and sale of sex, management of sex workers and brothels, and other activities related to sex work.'[86] It advises governments to make 'alliances' with 'managers and agents of sex workers' in order to encourage 'worker safety initiatives'. And so, NSWP's call to make brothel-keeping and pimping legal was included in a United Nations agency report.

Bingo.

That report is now a go-to reference for groups lobbying governments to make the prostitution trade entirely legal. Both the report and NSWP itself were cited by Amnesty International in its draft policy detailing why the organisation should back full decriminalisation of the sex trade.[87] 'Most significantly,' it stated, 'a large number of sex worker organisations and networks, including the Global Network of Sex Work Projects, support the decriminalisation of sex work.'[88]

Writing in defence of Amnesty's call for countries to decriminalise pimping and brothel-keeping, in 2015 the organisation's policy adviser insisted it was the right thing to do because 'questions about health, safety and equality under the law, are more important than any moral objection to the nature of sex work.'[89] In a similar vein, New Zealand's Prostitution Law Reform Committee maintained that their so-called decriminalised prostitution regime 'reflects [a] pragmatic sentiment, recognising that, even if viewed by some as undesirable, the practice of prostitution is likely to remain given ongoing levels of demand by men seeking to purchase sex.'[90] This kind of self-justifying fatalism is a particularly pernicious offshoot of the notion that issuing a 'how to' guide to brothel keepers is the best a government can do: the myth that there is no alternative.

The Sex Buyer Law

It is simply not equality that a man can buy a woman for the use of sex. That is not an equal society. Most of the girls that we get here are from other countries – Romania, Nigeria and so on. And a Swedish man on his way home from work stops by an eighteen-year-old Romanian girl and pays her 1,500 Swedish crowns to do whatever he wants with her for thirty minutes – that is simply not equality. That is not OK.

This was Detective Inspector Simon Häggström explaining to me at his office in Stockholm why he and his team are charged with tracking and arresting sex buyers. Before his current role in Stockholm Police's Prostitution Unit, Simon worked in the narcotics division. When the government's Kvinnofrid bill (which translates as 'women's peace') came into force in January 1999,[91] making Sweden the first country in the world where it was illegal to pay for sex but legal to receive payment for sex, Simon admits to being slightly bemused by it. 'I thought this was kind of a strange law: criminalise one part but not the other.' But the task of actually implementing the law soon opened his eyes to what was at stake. 'I just had to work with it for a few months and realised "Hey, of course we shouldn't criminalise these girls . . . we should help them." So I've totally changed my mind when it comes to the law. Today

I'm very supportive of it because I see it's working. I mean, it's definitely working.'

Securing this new prostitution law wasn't exactly a quick win for advocates. It followed decades of debate and consultation, with Sweden's Social Workers' Association proposing that criminalising paying for sex would 'improve equality between the sexes and prevent undue exploitation of socially deprived women'[92] in its response to a report commissioned by the Swedish government back in 1981. When it was finally adopted eighteen years later, the law's underlying principles – and its objective – were clear: prostitution is a form of violence against women that only exists because of male demand for the trade. That demand, and the institution of prostitution more widely, is a cause and a consequence of inequality between women and men, not an inevitable fact of life. The job of the state, then, is not to tolerate it, nor to regulate it, but to end it. Hence this 'abolitionist' approach is designed to target the perpetrators while supporting those they victimise. It's a three-pronged legal framework which criminalises paying for sex, decriminalises selling sex and provides support and exiting services for people exploited through prostitution. Known variously as the Nordic Model, Swedish Model or Sex Buyer Law, it's since been taken up by Iceland, Norway and Northern Ireland.* Needless to say, groups lobbying for pimping and brothel-keeping to be legal loathe it. According

* Canada criminalised paying for sex in 2014, and decriminalised selling sex in most circumstances. However, it remains a criminal offence to solicit in or next to a school ground, playground or daycare centre.

to the NSWP, it is 'a legal model based on ideology, misinformation, moralisation and a disregard for the agency, health, safety and wellbeing of sex workers'.[93] The appropriate term for the perspective underpinning it, they say, is 'fundamentalist feminist'.

What is inconvenient for groups wanting governments to enshrine brothel-keeping and pimping as legitimate jobs is that the effects of the Sex Buyer Law have so clearly exposed the fallacy of fatalism surrounding prostitution. Street prostitution in Sweden halved between 1999 and 2008, with the law's official evaluation finding no evidence it had merely been displaced.[94] Anonymous surveys conducted in 1996 and 2008 revealed that the proportion of men who pay for sex dropped from 12.7 to 7.6 per cent.[95] Added to which, in 2011 it was reported that the number of people involved in prostitution in Sweden – the country's 'prostitution population' – was approximately a tenth of Denmark's, where buying sex is legal. This was despite Sweden having 3.8 million more inhabitants than Denmark.[96]

The shrinking of the prostitution trade is also a trend that has been witnessed in Norway, which adopted the Sex Buyer Law in 2009. A government-commissioned evaluation published in 2014 reported that Oslo's street prostitution market had reduced by between 40 and 65 per cent.[97]

Crucially, public attitudes have changed substantially since the law was introduced in Sweden. In 1996, 45 per cent of women and just 20 per cent of men supported the legal principle of criminalising paying for sex. By 2008, 60 per cent of men and 79 per cent of women were behind it.[98] That attitude shift is at the heart of the Sex Buyer Law. Its presence on the statue book, and its enforcement on the ground, is about society collectively drawing a line in the sand that says to men and boys: when you have sex with someone, they should want to have sex with you. It's not a lofty ask, but a rock bottom requirement. It's simply not good enough that she just wants a drug fix – which you're effectively willing to finance if she agrees to have sex with you. It's not good enough that she's in debt to her trafficker or that she feels she has few other options. Handing over cash in order to get someone to agree to your sexual demands is sexual exploitation and society won't stand idly by while you do it; much less licence commercial venues dedicated to facilitating this abuse.

For Simon Häggström, it's no great puzzle why the Sex Buyer Law has had such an impact on the size of the prostitution trade. 'Many men buy sex simply because they can. And if there is a law saying no you cannot do this then most of the men will not do it. It's like driving against a red light,' he says. 'Why don't people drive against a red light even if there's no cars coming? Because it's illegal.' Simon recalls that when he made arrests while working in narcotics he would frequently face violence. Not so when arresting sex buyers. 'Most of them are just ordinary tax-paying men who live in a relationship with a family and buy sex on the way home from work – that's a typical sex buyer. So they would never dare to pick a fight with the police.' That's not to say the sex buyers he meets are relaxed about coming face to face with the police. 'They know that if the police catch them they might lose everything. In Sweden you have to understand the Swedish mindset on this: it is not socially acceptable to buy sex at all. This is something very shameful in Sweden to be arrested for . . . They will not fight us,' says Simon, 'but they will try to run away from us.'

Another effect of the Sex Buyer Law was explained to me by Detective Superintendent Kajsa Wahlberg, Sweden's national rapporteur on trafficking in human beings. The cash that sex buyers hand over, Kajsa says, 'is money that goes to organised crime activities mostly. It doesn't go to the women themselves.' There are huge profits at stake, she points out. 'One organisation recently here in Sweden, they brought women from Romania and one woman, she was [very popular with] buyers, they earned €70,000 a month on one woman. This is all money for organised crime . . . She didn't get any, it went to them. It's traffickers and pimps who benefit from prostitution, not the women. Very, very few women operate on their own.' Kajsa tells me that when police are on the scene, having tracked down a sex buyer at a hotel room, for instance, 'they will start to report this man for purchasing sex and while they are doing this, it takes some time, very frequently the pimp walks in and says, "What's going on?" And whoops! He's also being arrested.'

It is not just direct intercepts of pimps and traffickers that the Sex Buyer Law has facilitated. It has been found to have a deterrent effect on the trafficking of women into a country in the first place. Wire-tap evidence collected as part of po-

lice investigations after the law was adopted revealed traffickers viewed Sweden as a less attractive destination. The 2010
Swedish government evaluation noted, 'According to the National Criminal Police, it is clear that the ban on the purchase
of sexual services acts as a barrier to human traffickers and
procurers considering establishing themselves in Sweden.'[99]
Similarly, Norway's 2014 official review found a 'reduced
market and increased law enforcement posit larger risks for
human traffickers . . . The law has thus affected important
pull factors and reduced the extent of human trafficking in
Norway in comparison to a situation without a law.'[100] As a
result of its deterrent effect, in 2014 the Council of Europe
dubbed the Sex Buyer Law 'the most effective tool for preventing and combating trafficking in human beings'.[101]

Again, Simon Häggström points out that it's hardly surprising the law should have this deterrent effect. 'How will the
traffickers survive without sex buyers? The sex buyers are the
crucial sponsors of organised crime. The traffickers are not into
this because of sex . . . They are in this because of the money.'
Indeed, research into sex trafficking in south-eastern Europe
by the Austria-based NEXUS Institute to Combat Human
Trafficking highlighted that much of it was orchestrated by
organised groups who were often characterised by their 'man-
agerial approach' and, crucially, had 'the ability to respond to
(shifting) market demand.'[102] The authors found this was increasingly the case in Moldova, and Bosnia and Herzegovina:
'Traffickers are said to undertake informal market surveys to
identify the most advantageous market, calculating costs, risks

and benefits, and, once decided, they invest heavily in effectively penetrating their chosen markets.' The Sex Buyer Law markedly ups the risk for the potential 'customer base' traffickers are attempting to tap.

The Sex Buyer Law isn't a magic wand. Nobody claims that the mere act of adding it to the statute books will make the sex trade vanish. Like any piece of legislation, much of its potential is unlocked at the level of implementation. The Sex Buyer Law is a tool, and one that Sweden didn't make full use of immediately after its adoption, Kajsa Wahlberg tells me. The arrest rate was low, as was enthusiasm for it within the police. So, training on the use of the law was stepped up, and the arrest rate followed. 'We could have done that more quickly,' Wahlberg concedes. In 1999 there were just 10 convictions for paying for sex in Sweden; in 2010 there were 326.[103] The men convicted over the years have included the CEO of top security firm Securitas Sweden,[104] a chief public prosecutor,[105] and a judge from the highest court of appeal. The ultimate aim of the Sex Buyer Law, of course, is not to chalk up arrests and dish out fines, but to deter men from attempting to pay for sex in the first place. 'All men should know that if they even consider buying sex there is a risk of being caught and we do that by being visible in the media,' Simon Häggström explains.

So securing the Sex Buyer Law isn't a case of job done for campaigners. Instead, the task turns to prising open the full potential of the law, which sometimes includes pressing for amendments to the legislation itself. In Sweden, for instance, the maximum possible penalty for paying for sex was increased in 2011 from six months to one year's imprisonment to enable aggravating circumstances to be accounted for in sentencing, and there are now calls to make it a crime for Swedish citizens to pay for sex while travelling abroad (an extraterritoriality clause already in force in Norway).

Evidence of the profound social change that can be unlocked by the Sex Buyer Law is clear; its deterrent effect on sex buying and trafficking bust the myth of the sex trade's inevitability. Of all the different mixes of prostitution-related regulations in place around the world, the Sex Buyer Law is the only legal framework that has ending demand for prostitution – thereby ending this form of violence against women – as its objective.

By mandating and mobilising the state to end commercial sexual exploitation, the Sex Buyer Law poses an existential threat to the profitable exploits of pimps and brothel owners. Little wonder, then, that groups lobbying for laws that protect the right to extract third party profits from prostitution have been unremittingly hostile to the Sex Buyer Law. So, given the compelling evidence of its effectiveness, and the conversely damning official reports coming out of legalised and so-called decriminalised prostitution regimes, just what exactly are you meant to do if you want to stop the Sex Buyer Law being adopted?

The 'Activism and advocacy guide for challenging the "Swedish model"' published by the Netherlands-based International Committee on the Rights of Sex Workers in Europe explains that the key is to 'make the case that attempts to rescue and help sex workers have the opposite effect and do more harm than good'.[106] But how to do this? Especially given that on the pivotal accusation that the 'Swedish model' compounds the violence faced by women in prostitution, even this guide acknowledges 'there is no reliable study on the issue' to back it up. Well, if there's one take-home message from the campaigns for full decriminalisation of prostitution I've seen in action, it's that a lack of credible evidence needn't hold back efforts to smear the 'Swedish model'. Repeat claims often enough and they can take on the appearance of established fact. 'You may be able to raise doubt about the reliability of the evidence or the assumptions that your opponents use to make their case.'[107] Another tactic this how-to guide suggests: 'Blame the Opponent – For everything you possibly can!'

Underground

Central to the claims that 'attempts to rescue and help sex workers have the opposite effect and do more harm than good' is the charge that making paying for sex (and pimping and brothel-keeping) illegal drives prostitution 'underground' and that, whatever or wherever that is, it makes being paid for sex 'less safe'. Particular variants include allegations that it simply displaces prostitution, that it gives women less time to 'assess' police-wary sex buyers and thereby increases the risk of violence, and that it makes it harder for law enforcement and support services to identify and reach out to women involved in prostitution. Indeed, the charge that the Sex Buyer Law drives prostitution 'underground' has circulated since it was first introduced by Sweden, despite an official evaluation of its decade-long implementation concluding in 2010 that fears about prostitution being driven 'underground' 'have not been realised'.[108] Similarly, a 2014 evaluation in Norway commissioned by the Ministry of Justice and Public Security reported it '[did] not find any evidence of more violence against prostitutes after the ban on buying sex entered into force' and that the law had 'reduced demand'.[109] Aside from the lack of evidence, what is also remarkable about the political currency of claims prostitution is driven 'underground' is that the logic underpinning them, or, frequently, lack thereof, has so rarely been interrogated.

One such occasion, however, was during a formal hearing in 2014 of Northern Ireland's Justice Committee, which was deliberating whether to reform the country's prostitution laws. A representative of the International Union of Sex Workers (IUSW), invited to give evidence to the committee, claimed that women would be at greater risk of violence if the Sex Buyer Law was introduced in Northern Ireland: 'Because the buyers are now deemed criminals, the sex worker has less of an opportunity to assess her client when he pulls up to the kerb.'[110] Setting aside the fact that the sex buyer is *already* criminalised in this scenario because kerb-crawling is illegal in the UK, the claim does rather beg the question, what does a rapist look like? Perhaps they look like murderers, who can be easily discerned by – oh wait . . . Diane Martin CBE has spent almost twenty years providing support services to women involved in prostitution and is incredulous at the argument rolled out by IUSW. 'They say it doesn't give you time to check the punters out. What a joke. You don't get to check the punters out. You don't have time to interview men, give them a personality test, consult your crystal ball and do a police check! On the streets you might have a gut feeling now and then, but you may also be withdrawing from drugs or get battered by your "boyfriend" if you don't bring the money home for his drugs, so you will probably take that risk. In a flat or hotel room you have even less control – a locked door or other people hiding elsewhere.'

The reality, Diane told me, is that 'in prostitution you are the one vetted, you are the one assessed, and you are the one hoping to come out of it unharmed that night. So many punters are the man next door, the mild-mannered friendly guy who waves at his neighbours, pats his children on the head, finishes his nine-to-five and then drives over to the red light district, child car seats in the back. I have lost count of the violence doled out by "regulars" reported to me by women.' It's an assessment shared by Nozizwe Madlala-Routledge: 'I think it's this whole idea that a rapist looks like a monster or a man with horns or something. But it's an ordinary-looking person, and sometimes the people who you thought were decent until it was just the two of you [are not] . . . You can't assess them anyway, even if you had thirty minutes or you had a whole day.'

In the event, a member of the Justice Committee pointed out to the IUSW that one woman involved in prostitution is known to have been murdered in Sweden since the Sex Buyer Law was adopted (by her ex-partner; it was a domestic violence homicide). He continued: 'In Holland in the same period – of course, as you know, prostitution in Holland has been entirely legalised and is controlled – there have been 127 murders of prostitutes. Given those statistics, why would prostitutes be safer if you made it totally legal?'[111]*

'Given those statistics, I can see what you mean,' conceded the IUSW representative. But the organisation remained steadfast in alleging that criminalising paying for sex (while decriminalising selling sex) makes women more unsafe. In an apparent effort to ascertain exactly whose interests were being served by this testimony, the IUSW representative was asked about the nature of her group. The discussion was recorded in the official transcript of proceedings:[112]

Mr Wells [of the Committee of Justice]: Are there any pimps or those who profit from organising sexual services in your International Union of Sex Workers?

Ms Lee [of the IUSW]: Some of the members are managers, yes.

Mr Wells: So, they are pimps.

---

* The Netherlands has a population of approximately 16.9 million, while Sweden's population is 9.8 million. On the basis of the figures cited by the Justice Committee, per head of total population there are over 70 times more murders of women in prostitution in the Netherlands.[113]

Ms Lee: Well, if you want to use that term, yes.

Mr Wells: So, it is not just a union of sex workers; it is also those who control sex workers.

Ms Lee: Yes.

Despite the evidence of the Sex Buyer Law's impact in Sweden contradicting Lee's claims, the IUSW spokesperson maintained that she could speak with authority because 'I have found myself in the position – I do not know whether you would call it fortunate or unfortunate – of becoming the voice for sex workers in Ireland.' On this, the committee again dug a little deeper.

Chairperson: You say that you speak for the vast majority. I am trying to quantify that. Can you tell me how many sex workers you purport to speak for?

Ms Lee: In the UK, because it is such a clandestine industry in some regards, statistics are hard to come by, but the estimates are that there are 80,000 sex workers in the UK. That is across the broad spectrum and includes webcam strippers etc.

Chairperson: Are they are all members of your international union?

Ms Lee: No, they are not.

Chairperson: So, how many members does the International Union of Sex Workers have?

Ms Lee: I am not entirely sure about that. I would have to look that up and come back to you.

Chairperson: It is just that you said that you speak for the vast majority.

Ms Lee: Yes.

Chairperson: I am trying to establish the credibility of the organisation that you purport to represent. That is important, because, obviously, we will refer to this evidence session, and we need to know that what you have said comes from a credible organisation. So, how many members are there in the International Union of Sex Workers?

Ms Lee: I would need to check that out and come back to you.

Lee did later report back to the committee: 'She's provided that information indicating it's a small closed organisation of ten individuals, none of whom are based in Northern Ireland.'[114]

One of the off-shoots of Lee's claim finds expression in the Open Society Foundations' run-down of 'Ten reasons to decriminalize sex work'. This report alleges, 'Rather than ending demand for sex work, penalties on clients force sex workers to provide services in clandestine locations, which increases the risk of violence.'[115] I put this claim to Alan Caton, former detective superintendent of Suffolk Constabulary (UK). 'I don't think it can ever be made safe,' he said resolutely. Caton was tasked with overhauling his force's approach to prostitution after five young women were murdered in Ipswich in 2006 by a local sex buyer, Steve Wright. '[Wright] was somebody who was known to these women. So a lot of these women felt it was safe. He was a regular. And that in itself just goes to show that even people that come across as being regulars and safe for whatever reason can carry out heinous criminal acts as Steve Wright did on five young women in Ipswich.'

When it came to drawing up Suffolk's new policing strategy, continuing to tacitly tolerate the prostitution trade was not an option for Caton. Nor was embarking on a quest to find the apocryphal 'clean safe place' for women to be abused in. 'I think it couldn't be more dangerous for women who predominantly are addicted to drugs and alcohol, who are out on the streets getting in cars of men that they don't know.' Instead, his team mounted an 'end demand' approach to prostitution. They cracked down on kerb-crawling (which was already illegal) and diverted women away from the criminal justice system, working with local agencies to support them to exit. The impact was stark. An evaluation by the University of East Anglia of the strategy's first four years found 'clear and sustained success' in 'eliminating kerb crawlers from the streets' and 'developing routes out' for women involved in the trade.[116] There was no evidence the trade had merely been displaced. 'If you do put the right emphasis on support and you are tackling the demand you can actually change people's behaviour and not displace it elsewhere – which was certainly the case in Ipswich,' says Caton. (While the Ipswich strategy drew on the fundamental principles of the Sex Buyer Law, its impact on the trade was ultimately curtailed by not actually having this law on the statute books. Because paying for sex wasn't a crime, police weren't able to instigate an 'end demand' approach to prostitution in off-street locations, where the majority of sex buyers opt to hand over money.)

I put another of the claims – that criminalising paying for sex (while decriminalising selling sex) simply makes it harder for police and support services to identify women in prostitution – to Detective Inspector Simon Häggström. He'd heard it before, and was clearly frustrated by rumours that surround the Sex Buyer Law, which he encounters when travelling abroad to share his team's experiences of implementing the legislation. 'Critics are saying that the police in Sweden are no longer able to find [indoor, internet-advertised] prostitution – which is actually bullshit.' Why? 'Because buyers and sellers need to find each other,' Häggström says. 'The sex buyers sit in front of their computers and go to a site to find an advertisement and if the sex buyer can do that then of course police can do the same. It's not that hard. So finding prostitution is not a problem for us.' Detective Superintendent Kajsa Wahlberg similarly finds the logic of the claim wanting. She told an assembled audience of law enforcement officials at a conference in the Netherlands: 'Those who are critical [of] the legislation are often accusing the Swedish police of pushing prostitution activities underground. I want to underline that prostitution activities are not and cannot be pushed underground. The profit of traffickers, procurers and other prostitution operators is obviously dependent on [men being able to] access women who they wish to purchase for prostitution purposes. If law enforcement agencies want to find out where prostitution activities takes place, the police can.'[117]

Overground

Attempting to ward off countries from adopting the Sex Buyer Law by conjuring up a foreboding (as well as unevidenced and often illogical) image of a prostitution trade that's invisible, out of reach, *underground*, implies a contra picture that's apparently preferable.

So what exactly does this visible, in-reach, *overground* prostitution trade look like?

Does it look like mega-brothels? These ultra visible, multi-story, commercial landmarks are now a feature of Germany's legal prostitution trade. And in 2012, Auckland council in New Zealand gave the go-ahead for the construction of a multi-storey 'super-brothel'.*[118] Is this the kind of 'visible' we're supposed to be aiming for?

Or how about Amsterdam's window brothels? A sector in which the women paid to have sex are literally on public view; where tourists, local residents, police and would-be sex buyers can all get a good look; where, the Dutch Government reports, 'the great majority' of women have a pimp.[119] Are we getting closer?

* Ultimately, legal wranglings with a competitor over a liquor licence reportedly put the millionaire brothel business owners off embarking on their green-lighted building project.

Perhaps women in prostitution could be kept within the state's reach (and fulfil their legal obligations as 'self-employed workers') using the same system they operate in the German city of Bonn. There, women waiting on the street for unknown men to pull up in their cars and request sex acts have to buy a 'tax ticket' for €6 each night from a machine on the street.[120] Is that what 'overground' prostitution looks like?

The reality is, highly visible, above-board prostitution systems don't erase the harm; they hide it in plain sight. The failed attempts by states to expunge the harms inherent and attendant to prostitution by operating a visible, legal, 'overground' sex trade only confirm in practice what should be abundantly clear in principle: there is not, nor will there ever be, a 'safe place' for people to be abused in.

MYTH 6: Resistance is futile

So here we are. Behind us, the sex trade's march into the mainstream. Before us, a choice: accept that this will be an age in which society functions within cultural and legal lines laid out by pimps and pornographers, or don't.

Cut through the myths and it's clear the sex trade is a phenomenon entirely of our own creation: industrial-scale commercial sexual exploitation, born of sex inequality, and midwifed by third-party profiteers – profiteers whose exploits get a helping hand from factors like abuse, neglect, racism and poverty. We made this. We can unmake it.

And yet here we face another myth: that while in principle the sex trade is not inevitable, in practice it is simply too big, too powerful, too profitable to stop. Discussing public concerns about pornography, Professor John Naughton, vice-president of Wolfson College, Cambridge, has argued that meaningful action to tackle it is a 'non-starter, for two reasons: first, there's a huge market/appetite for it; and second, too many powerful agencies have a vested interest in supplying it.'[1] To point out that this is self-fulfilling defeatism is not to deny that the barriers to change will be substantial, however. And they won't always lie where you might expect.

There is no getting around the fact, for instance, that high profile individuals and groups whose identities are bound up with women's rights have openly championed sex trade myths. They have publicly pushed for policies that categorise sexual abuse as legitimate consumer behaviour. For them to acknowledge this could feel pretty embarrassing, to say the least. Take the Association for Women's Rights in Development (AWID), an influential voice in the international arena. They publicly backed the NSWP and partners when they (unsuccessfully) lobbied the European Parliament in 2014 to oppose the Sex Buyer Law.[2] Mama Cash, an Amsterdam-based women's rights funder, is host to the Red Umbrella Fund – a global money pot for groups advancing the 'sex work is work'[3] agenda. (Organisations wanting to end prostitution are told not to bother applying.[4]) Then there's Amnesty International, whose leadership voted in 2015 to tell countries to decriminalise pimping, brothel-keeping and sex buying. According to Amnesty's secretary general, this was 'for the protection of the human rights of sex workers'.[5] 'Bravo!' tweeted AWID in response.[6]

This represents a special kind of win for proponents of unbridled sex trade profiteering. Because while you might reasonably expect that, on a personal level, the cognitive dissonance that advocating this generates in people who champion feminism would be sufficient to prompt a rethink, the counter-intuitive point about cognitive dissonance is that it can harden inconsistent attitudes. The sheer contradiction between believing in women's equality while publicly legitimising men's treatment of them as subordinate sex objects means the level of discomfort involved in acknowledging this can make people go to great lengths not to have to do so. Psychologists Philip Zimbardo and Michael Leippe note that when a person publicly commits to a position and is then confronted by a contradictory view, they 'develop less, not more, openness to it. Cognitive responses will be increasingly hostile to the message.'[7] In short, for some, the urge to cling to sex trade myths in order to save face will be immense. Consider what it will take for Amnesty International to reverse its framing of prostitution as 'sex work' and to make a volte-face on its call for pimping and brothel-keeping to be legal. The level of institutional failure necessary to produce that recommendation is so great that the reputation of the individuals responsible for it, and their positions within the organisation, are likely at stake. It will take considerable internal leadership to acknowledge what's gone wrong and to redress the damage inflicted on the organisation's credibility, let alone its contribution to the struggle for women's rights.

There will be no shortage of phoney solutions wheeled out in response to calls for change, either. Initiatives designed to placate concerns but preserve the profits of pimps, brothel owners and pornographers. (And, of course, preserve the 'right' to pay for sexual access to another person.) Ethical porn! Ethical strip clubs! ('Ethical brothels!' would likely be a harder sell.) 'Appeal to people's rights to be able to consume,' advised Diane Duke, representative of the Free Speech Coalition – the US porn industry's trade association – who was dishing out advice to UK colleagues at the XBIZ EU conference I attended in 2013. This particular session was on how to resist the 'war on porn'. 'People get pissed off when you take away their porn,' she said. And so, those same users could be used to help bankroll defence of the industry. 'You guys have big lists. I know when they come to your sites they don't want to think about politics, but there may just be a flash up that says "your porn is in danger".' Another speaker recommended that 'people in the sex industry campaign for sex education and put some money together for that'. This, it was suggested, could be great for 'taking the moral highground back a bit'. If you're teaching kids that that is Planet Porn, and this is Planet Earth, and what they just have to do is remember that it's 'fantasy', then this kind of 'education' could reinforce sex trade myths (as well as being a boon for porn industry PR). So as a proposed act of charity, it was a pretty good business idea given the context.

Then there'll be the inevitable heckling from the sidelines: that one particular law you're currently proposing won't solve absolutely everything all at once so it's completely pointless! There's no way it could possibly work! You'll just make things worse!

But the scaremongering, the false solutions; these are hardly insurmountable barriers. No, change will not happen all at once. Yes, there will be important discussions about the best strategies for delivering it. But the sex trade is not an inevitable feature of the twenty-first century. The six central myths tackled by this book are prevalent now, but here are six weak points in the system propping up pimps and pornographers.

Push on them hard enough, and you can collapse the global sexual exploitation trade.

1. The sex trade is reliant on mainstream institutions, but they are not reliant on it.

In May 2015, porn magnate Fabian Thylmann visited the Oxford Union. I sat in the audience as the Manwin founder argued for the debate proposition, 'This house embraces sex work as a career choice', and on my way out spotted him waiting in the courtyard. I took the opportunity to ask Thylmann what he thought posed the biggest threat to the porn industry. 'It's banks,' he said. There's this strange public perception, Thylmann told me, that 'handling money of porn companies is evil. So the porn industry has a lot more to deal with in terms of handling their finances and transactions.' His response points to a critical feature of the sex trade: it is not a self-sufficient, self-contained entity, impervious to the actions of others. It is a trade dependent on 'mainstream' institutions to keep the profits flowing. Institutions like banks, credit card companies, high-street retailers, and, of course, governments. And while the sex trade is propped up by these institutions, they, in turn, are not ultimately beholden to it. They may currently profit from the association, but for them it is a marriage of convenience. If it were to become too uncomfortable, if these institutions were actually held to public account for the enabling role they play in sexual exploitation, they would have to drop their support for pimps and pornographers.

In 2013 UK Feminista and Object launched a campaign against lads' mags because of the sexually objectifying images they peddled. But the target for our protest wasn't lads' mags publishers. It was supermarkets. We knew that if a bunch of placard-waving feminists turned up outside the offices of *Nuts* and *Zoo*, it would far more likely inspire amusement than any kind of Damascene moment for those inside. (One particular lads' mag, *Maxim*, had previously published a feature on 'How to cure a feminist: turn an unshaven, militant, protesting vegan into an actual girl!'[8]) The supermarkets that stocked them, however, were less likely to find it funny. They had family-friendly brands to protect. And lads' mags were obviously just one of a multitude of products stocked by the stores. They could afford to be dumped.

So we targeted Tesco, the UK's biggest retailer, ensuring its brand was firmly in the spotlight. Tactics included protests outside Tesco stores, lobbying shareholders at their AGM, and publishing legal advice showing stocking lads' mags could constitute sexual harassment or sex discrimination (in relation to staff and customers). Activists also mobilised online, lobbying supermarkets to #losetheladsmags. Within twenty-four hours of our tweeting at Tesco executives, they publicly pledged to take action; within three days (we didn't stop tweeting) they agreed to meet us. Three months into the campaign, Tesco age-restricted lads' mags. Four months in, the Co-operative dropped them altogether from their 4,000 stores.

Less than a year after Lose the Lads' Mags was launched, the parent company of *Nuts* magazine, IPC Media, announced they were closing it down. Pete Cashmore, who had worked at *Nuts* since its launch ten years earlier, later wrote:

> The official reason given was that the magazine was losing money hand over fist, but we believed this to be so much hooey – we were still the dominant title in the men's market, shifting 200,000 copies a month and still beating our immediate rivals *Zoo* every week without fail. We were also one of the dominant titles on smartphones and tablets, and here I'm not just talking about in the men's sector, I'm talking across all titles – basically, we'd nailed the interactive format very quickly and so were duking it out with the big boys, the tech titles and broadsheets. Nope, even though we were never explicitly told it, it was obvious we'd become more trouble than we were worth – we'd spent the last two years being constantly pilloried by the pressure group UK Feminista, their various beneficiaries and their Lose the Lads' Mags campaign, and found ourselves in the press as much for our supposed misogyny, an accusation which always baffled me (the only people we were ever mean about, or objectified, were ourselves), as we did for showcasing Holly from *Geordie Shore*'s bold new look.[9]

The porn trade's dependency on the risk calculation made by companies in their supply chain was again alluded to by Fabian Thylmann during a 2012 industry conference. He revealed that Playboy had offered his corporation the chance to buy their online assets. But it wasn't Playboy's website Thyl-mann wanted. 'I told them, look, it's nice and so on, playboy. com – what you have online, but what I really want is your TV assets.'[10] Why? Because it would be his Trojan horse (or rabbit). A way to get his other hardcore porn productions into mainstream media. '[Playboy TV] gives us a way to get into the door of people like Google, of people like Samsung's internet TV group, of people like Netflix.' When it came to his other porn brands, Thylmann explained,

If we knock on Netflix's door they just tell us to turn around and leave because they don't want this content. Or at least they feel they don't want this content because they are afraid of it. They are not afraid of Playboy. Everybody loves Playboy. It's nice and clean, perfect, lovely. They'll take it. At least, they can be convinced to take it and actually talk to us about it. So it's a nice first step in getting them to do a deal. And later on, I can always start pushing other products into the whole mix, or at least use some of our content on the Playboy TV brands then use on Netflix and so on.

Despite protracted negotiations, Thylmann secured the deal with Playboy. 'It was a very, very important transaction for me.'

Pimps and pornographers are not out of reach. Their prof-iteering is balanced on top of a heap of other companies and institutions. Some help prop up the trade through action, others through inaction. But ending commercial sexual exploitation will require ensuring they pull their enabling role.

2. *The sex trade needs men to regurgitate its myths or keep quiet.*

Boys will be boys, so sex trade fans tell us. But Tom Meagher is one of a growing number of men working to publicly put the lie to this message. I met Tom in the European Parliament at an event on tackling violence against women. He was there on behalf of White Ribbon Ireland, a group dedicated to mobilising men to take action to end violence against women, and which is among those pushing for the Sex Buyer Law to be adopted in Ireland. I later asked Tom what had prompted him to get involved in efforts to end sexist violence, and prostitution in particular. 'In 2012, my wife Jill was raped and murdered on her way home from a night out in Melbourne, Australia,' he replied.

My reaction to this – apart from all the trauma and grief that accompanied such a sudden and painful loss – was to study the motivations of her murderer, Adrian Bayley. What stood out for me was not necessarily his deviance, but his deep-rooted misogyny. What stood out even more on further study was the fact that, although his cruelty was extraordinary and thankfully rare, his misogyny, and the words he used to express it, were not. My perception slowly shifted from seeing this individual as the embodiment of evil, to seeing his actions, his attitudes

and his misogyny as the evils that motivate a larger
spectrum of violence against women in wider society.

I remember, as I studied him further, reading a court
report from 2002 that documented a litany of particularly
violent rapes of prostituted women [that Bayley had been
convicted of]. When questioned by the police about why
he had done it, he replied, 'I paid for her, I can do what I
want with her.'

Tom had then dug deeper into research on sex buyers, which
'revealed similar attitudinal patterns of othering and dehumanisation [of] the women they have bought. I wouldn't
suggest that all sex buyers commit the same acts of evil as
Bayley did, but they expressed a dismissal of the agency of the
women they bought, often coupled with a feeling of being
ripped off if that agency was expressed by the woman refusing
certain sex acts.' Tom now campaigns alongside survivors of
prostitution for the Sex Buyer Law – something he believes
will be a 'game-changer in terms of men's attitude to women
in general.'

He is also adamant that more men need to speak out. 'Men
make the sex trade exist by their demand that women's bodies
be commodities in the marketplace. The sex trade is directed
by men and money. I think we have to be very clear that men
need to take responsibility for the harms that exist within
it. If not for our actual involvement, for our ambivalence to
the misogyny that underpins it.' The need to challenge this
ambivalence lead to Tom's involvement in We Don't Buy It,

a campaign in Ireland calling on men to take a stand against prostitution and trafficking.[11] 'I can certainly envision a world without the sex trade,' he said. 'There is absolutely nothing inevitable about the existence of a sex trade. I think it will take legal and social measures to divest it of the myths that surround it.'

Occasionally, we hear from men who expose the toxic sense of entitlement behind demand for the sex trade somewhat more inadvertently than initiatives like White Ribbon Ireland. In 2013, a 'Manifesto of the 343 bastards' was published in the French press. The signatories' rallying cry, 'Touche pas à ma pute!' ('Hands off my whore!'),[12] was directed at the French government, which at the time was trying to pass the Sex Buyer Law (to decriminalise selling sex and criminalise paying for sex).

The 343 men declared that most of them 'have been, go to or will go to prostitutes',[13] and included high-profile figures, including Dominique Strauss-Kahn's lawyer, Richard Malka, who defended the former head of the International Monetary Fund against charges of aggravated pimping.[14] The format of the 'manifesto' was a reference to a feminist protest in 1971, when 343 women, including Simone de Beauvoir, petitioned the French government to legalise abortion. They were referred to in the press as 'the 343 bitches'.[15]

The Manifesto of the 343 Bastards backfired, however, prompting a national outcry and headlines around the world. The French minister for women's rights at the time, Najat Vallaud-Belkacem, hit back, pointing out that the 343 women had 'demanded to be able to freely decide what to do with their bodies' while the 343 men 'demand the right to decide what to do with the bodies of others'.[16]

Grégoire Théry, who has been involved with the French organisation Mouvement du Nid's campaign for the Sex Buyer Law for many years, told me that the petition by the 343 men 'was a pure expression of something which was a bit less conscious but very present in people's minds: that men have a right to it, they have a right [to] women's bodies. But the fact that it was written down shocked a lot of people.' The Manifesto of the 343 Bastards ended up being a boost for their opponents precisely because the real driver of the sex trade was on public show, rather than obscured behind myths. It was a flat-out, 'honest' assertion of sex buyers' sense of entitlement to pay to access women's bodies. For Théry, it represented 'the direct and unashamed expression of something very strong but which can't be said'. Rare as its open declaration may be, the belief among some that men have a right to pay to sexually access women is there beneath the surface. Expose it and you expose the roots of the sex trade.

3. Setting limits to the market is hardly revolutionary. The effect will be.

'Our own view', wrote Tim Worstall of the Adam Smith Institute, 'is that what consenting adults get up to is up to consenting adults.'[17] So prostitution should be fully legalised, he concluded. The Adam Smith Institute's mission is 'to promote libertarian and free market ideas',[18] and Worstall seems

perplexed by the suggestion that governments should criminalise paying for sex, that 'liberty and freedom should be
limited when cash changes hands'.

Setting aside what's being traded for a moment, this idea
that market exchanges are merely a series of disconnected,
private transactions, with government's only legitimate role
being to *protect* that exchange with the 'full majesty of the
law'[19] (as Worstall proposes for the prostitution trade), was
not one shared by his think tank's name-sake. Philosopher
Debra Satz points out that 'Smith's insights and economic
perspective cannot easily be summed up by a single principle
of free exchange between consenting adults.'[20] Instead, she
viewed the market as 'a complex heterogeneous institution',
says Satz, and believed 'the effects of a particular market on
the structure of political power and on human development
are relevant to its assessment'. Recognising that markets are
inextricably intertwined with society is fundamental to how
we organise today, as is the notion that they do not trump social justice. We cannot contract away our basic human rights;
they still apply. Nor can you buy the right to violate someone
else's. Hence, when it comes to the sexually abusive act of co-
ercing someone to have sex by offering them money, the fact
that a punter has paid to do it obviously does not (or should
not) buy him exemption from societal prohibitions against
sexual abuse.

There is a panoply of items and activities that societies
have decided cannot be bought or sold: human organs, votes,
bonded labour, child labour and so on. And for a host of rea-

sons: because of unavoidable harm to those involved, because of the risk of exploitation of the most vulnerable, because it clashes with the very principles of equality and democracy, let alone their practical realisation. Paying a person for sex acts, and third-party profiteering from it, is commercial sexual exploitation. And it's high time it took its rightful place on the list of things labelled not for sale.

4. Laws against pimping apply to pimps with cameras.

Psst. Listen up. There's a little-known method of turning a criminal act into a legal one: film it. Want to legally turn a profit on someone else's kidney? Film them having it removed. Perhaps you're a banker who wants to engage in a bit of market manipulation without the possibility of legal hassle. If so, just film the transactions being made; call it an expression of your financial artistry. Just set up a camera, do the transactions and, oh, wait. The mere act of filming an illegal activity obviously does not magic it into a legal one. And yet the pornography industry has been pulling off this farce for decades.

As I've argued, pornography is filmed prostitution. Many countries already prohibit third parties from facilitating or profiting from someone else's prostitution. (The motivations may vary between countries, but it can clearly provide principle and practical recognition that third-party profiteering from another person being paid for sex is commercial sexual exploitation and further fuels the demand for it.) Now, if a person arranges and/or profits from someone else's prostitution, the fact that there was a camera present filming the prostitution does not alter the basic fact that *they arranged and/ or profited from someone else's prostitution*. Those involved may prefer terms like 'agent' over 'pimp', but that's hardly surprising. So why aren't laws against third-party profiteering from prostitution applied to the filmed prostitution trade?

I spoke to lawyers to find out the answer to this question, and it became increasingly apparent that the reasons are historical and political, rather than legal and logical. Pornographers have been highly effective in directing public debate towards the fact that they use media to disseminate their product, and consequently drawing on legal principles around freedom of speech. But the fact that pornographers make use of media in order to facilitate profit-making is beside the point when considering the legality of the act in question: exploiting someone else's prostitution for commercial gain. Just as it would be beside the point when considering the legality of profiting from the removal of someone else's kidney whether or not the operation was filmed and disseminated (and masturbated to).

McAllister Olivarius is an international law firm that specialises in representing victims of so-called 'revenge porn' (where nude or sexually explicit images of a person are shared without their permission). I asked Dr Ann Olivarius, senior partner at the firm, what she thought about redressing the inconsistency in how third-party prohibitions against profiteering from prostitution are enforced – by applying them to pornographers. 'No country in the world has yet adopted effective laws to deal with the porn industry and the increasing harm it is causing,' she said. '[This] new approach is brilliant and makes legal sense. I would like to see it translated into real policy in the UK and elsewhere.'

Despite the inevitable scaremongering, the implications of applying laws against third-party profiteering clearly wouldn't prohibit the act of people filming themselves having sex, or sharing the footage. Who it would apply to is *profiteers* facilitating and exploiting someone else's *prostitution*. Commercial sexual exploitation is still commercial sexual exploitation if someone is stood there holding a camera. The challenge ahead is for feminist lawyers and activists to build the political will and awareness to reflect this in how laws are enforced.

5. A growing movement is demanding change.

In spite of the hostility frequently meted out to detractors, a burgeoning global movement is fighting back; people whose courage to speak out against the sex trade is matched only by their compassionate resolve to prevent others being exploited in the future. Sometimes at significant personal cost.

'When I was in that situation and isolated, I longed to be seen, for someone to notice that something was wrong, to ask the right questions.' Diane Martin CBE explained to me how, since getting out of prostitution, she has spent nearly twenty years working to 'take those experiences and transform them into a response that reaches out to other women, to be those seeing eyes, to ask those questions to girls at risk and women involved'. Diane is now at the forefront of efforts in the UK to secure the Sex Buyer Law, and is certainly under no illusions about the battle campaigners have on their hands. 'The sex trade is a billion dollar industry and the greed of those making money off the backs of mainly economically and socially disadvantaged women will not unclench their fists easily.'

The challenges can also be more personal. Speaking in 2014 at the launch of End Demand, a UK campaign for the Sex Buyer Law, Diane told the assembled audience at the Houses of Parliament what it had been like preparing to speak to them about her experiences in the sex trade: 'I was still surprised to encounter the depth of emotion as well as how my body still responded in the remembering: shaking, crying, nausea, confusion, dizziness. There is always a cost in the remembering, there is always a cost in the telling.'[21] Yet she was resolute. 'I want to see the Sex Buyer Law introduced because it is the demand that fuels the exploitation that is the sex industry. I want it near impossible for organised crime, pimps and punters to operate here. I want to be part of a society that rejects the idea that people are for sale and I want us to be part of a bigger picture that sees this model adopted globally.'

Since Jessie decided to leave the pornography trade, she has faced the very personal challenge of having to confront an industry that still refuses to let go of her. 'They're constantly trying to market my films even though I've been out of it for almost a year and a half now,' Jessie tells me. 'And I get so upset when I blog on my twitter and they're like, "oh, check out this scene with [my name]." I'm just like, stop. I don't wanna see that anymore.' Nonetheless, she has chosen to speak out publicly against the trade 'for that fifteen-, sixteen-year-old girl that I used to be . . . I just really want to get the message out there because like I said I feel like I had an advantage of really seeing what the porn industry was like.'

The resistance faced by those working to abolish the sex trade can sometimes simply be the quiet brute force of mass indifference, or even bemusement that someone should be trying to stand in the industry's path. Inge Hauschildt-Schön, a retired teacher, has encountered both of these responses. In the autumn of 2014, Inge drove me the short distance from her home in Germany to a local business park. There, amid car dealerships and repair shops, was the focus of her nearly decade-long campaign: the 'Erotic Island', a legal fifteen-room brothel. (The brothel is located right next to a highway junction, providing maximum convenience and discretion for punters when paying a visit.)

Inge first read about plans to open the brothel in her local newspaper, back in 2005. 'We thought that is a scandal, that that should happen here. The scandal was that I know what prostitution means.' Inge had her 'feminist awakening' during the 1970s, she told me, after her husband bought her a copy of the German feminist magazine, *EMMA*. There was no question for Inge of sitting back as plans for a brothel ploughed ahead in her town. 'If the body of a woman is sold as something you can buy, as a consumer item, and men can do with the openings of that consumer item everything they want to do,' then this, she said, 'is inhuman and it is violence'. For Inge, the real question is, 'how is it possible that a civil society looks away?' So, she and a group of fellow residents did everything they could think of to make people really look: from a petition to public meetings to protest.

Rather than outrage, however, their campaign, called Marburger Bürgerinitiative bi-gegen-bordell (Marburg Citizens' Initiative against the brothel)[22] initially prompted sneers from the local press and council officials. It was clear to Inge, who was seventy-five years old when we met, that her age was being used as a way to dismiss her arguments. 'They said, "Oh, those old women, why do they fight against prostitution? It's quite clear it is because they are old." Well, I was shocked, though today I can laugh about it.'

Despite growing support for their cause, in 2007 the mayor gave a green light to the brothel. 'We were really angry,' Inge recalls, but 'we decided not to give up.' Since then, the group has helped campaigners in other parts of Germany resist plans for new brothels and successfully lobbied to stop another nearby brothel advertising 'flat-rate sex', which meant, Inge explained, 'you can have as many women as you want to, you can do with these women what you want to, and there is a flat rate: €29.' After Inge's press statement condemning flat-rate promotion was splashed across the media, the brothel's owner called Inge's house to ask what all the fuss was about. 'I explained to him why I protested against this thing.' Her protest worked. 'He stopped,' she says coolly.

Sustaining the campaign over the past nine years hasn't been easy. 'To see the inhumanity even in your surroundings, this is difficult to bear . . . It is really sad. You think you live in a civil country, and these things happen. I wouldn't really have thought that that is possible, but it is. And I can't really believe that such a lack of empathy when you talk about that.' But the prospect of the alternative, remaining silent, is worse. 'When you see the other side – these hundreds of thousands of women who suffer, I can't understand why people don't want to hear of that and to see that and to do anything against that.' Inge knows that change doesn't often happen overnight, but in persevering, in finding the fortitude to keep speaking up, she and her fellow activists are disrupting the message that the presence of government-sanctioned brothels in the town is somehow normal and acceptable. They are part of a growing movement in Germany that has come together in an initiative called Stop Sexkauf, determined to get the Sex Buyer Law on to the statute books and see the Government finally acknowledge that, as Inge puts it, 'this inhumanity cannot be legalised'.

Five months after meeting Inge, I was sitting with Nozizwe Madlala-Routledge in the Cape Town offices of her organisation, Embrace Dignity. I asked Madlala-Routledge what it was that kept her going in the campaign to end commercial sexual exploitation, a campaign frequently met with hostility and ridicule. 'When I joined the liberation struggle against apartheid,' she replied, 'many of us, in fact, the majority did not believe that we could end apartheid in our lifetimes. I remember there was a slogan popularised by Oliver Tambo, saying "end apartheid in our lifetime", and we used to say that slogan but we didn't really believe it was possible. I believe it is possible to end prostitution, just like it was possible to end apartheid.' Madlala-Routledge is in no doubt about the potential for change because we 'have a movement that is growing in strength, that is calling for the abolition of prostitution. I feel that we all have a part in that movement.'

6. 'The future belongs to those who believe in the beauty of their dreams.'

There were echoes of this adage, widely attributed to Eleanor Roosevelt,[23] in the confident resolve of the many campaigners I met while researching this book. They know that however much control the sex trade currently wields, however big the profits, they are in the infinitely more advantageous position of fighting for justice. So when confronted by myths shielding the short-term rewards sought by pimps and sex buyers, they know their vision of an equal future – free of the violence that is the sex trade – is simply more powerful, more beautiful. It's what Madlala-Routledge explained helps fix her resolve: 'The feeling that you are actually on the right side of history.'

It was her vision of a future in which there is no longer demand for the sex trade that inspired fifty-seven-year-old Rosen Hircher to set off on an 800-kilometre walk across France in the autumn of 2014. Starting in Saintes, the town near Bordeaux where she was first paid for sex, and ending in Paris, the last place she was ever paid for sex, Rosen was protesting against the French Senate stalling a government bill to introduce the Sex Buyer Law. 'I went through prostitution myself and thus I knew the violence that women in prostitution went through,' Rosen explained to me when we met in Paris the following year. 'I really thought we have to move right now. It's time to act.' Rosen's Marche Pour L'Abolition[24] had a galvanising effect, prompting news headlines and public shows of support from politicians. France's minister for women's rights, Pascale Boistard, joined Rosen for the final leg of the march.

'The marching in itself was a pleasure. It was a pleasure to walk all the day long.' Rosen had run marathons in her youth, and the main preparation she did for her 500-mile hike was psychological, not physical. 'The body remembers,' she told me.

Rosen exited the prostitution trade in 2009 having entered it twenty-two years earlier. She explained it was a confluence of events that had led to her involvement. 'According to my own analysis, there is the separation between my parents and the kidnapping [of me] by my father, [and] sexual abuse – I was thirteen – by my uncle. From nine to seventeen I went through everything that can make a young girl become a good prostitute.' Shortly before turning eighteen Rosen left home. While hitching a ride she was picked up by two men who turned out to be involved in a pimping network. Rosen ended up getting married to one of them. 'So [the marriage] saved me from the street at the time when I was eighteen . . . But it also got me to prostitution in the end.' Rosen's sixteen years of marriage were, she says, 'just brackets'. 'In the end I did what I was trained for and I fell eventually in prostitution. And I stayed twenty-two years. There is always an event in your past for all women in prostitution. There is always an event in the past that caused you to go into prostitution.'

While recalling the last day of her march, Rosen's eyes started to fill with tears. She struggled to get the words out as she remembered meeting a group of young women who had travelled to Paris to cheer her on. The women had previously been trafficked into the sex trade, and were there with the supporting organisation, Mouvement du Nid. 'I'm always crying when I come back to this. I cry for the good moments . . . [The women] had suffered in prostitution but were standing up and proud of being here and joining me for the final day of my march.'

Arriving in Paris wasn't the end of Rosen's campaigning, however. Once the Sex Buyer Law is adopted the task will turn to keeping it ('there will automatically be a backlash', she predicts) and ensuring it is fully implemented. Rosen told me she feels 'better and better' about the future, but is under no illusions about how long, and at times difficult, the journey ahead will be – both for the campaign and for her personally. The impact of being in prostitution was as if she 'had no body and no more feelings also. You lose your perceptions of life and death'. And that has only recently started to change. 'Laughing or crying – it's coming back, I feel it . . . I can't know when I will completely get back those feelings, emotions and physical sensations.' Part of her is nervous about this happening. 'There is this fear of really exiting prostitution and also exiting this absence of perceptions, sensations, feelings etc., because that's also what protects us and allows and allows us to stand up. And thus we want to feel again, and you are afraid of feeling again because you are afraid of what you will feel.'

Yet Rosen remains fixed on changing the law so it recognises prostitution as violence against women – decriminalising the 'selling' but criminalising the 'buying' of sex acts. 'It will be a revolution, to me.'

During Rosen's Marche Pour L'Abolition, members of the public rallied to support her call for change. On social media they used the hashtag #EnMarcheAvecRosen. It was one of the best parts of the journey, says Rosen: 'Knowing that thousands of people were walking with me.'

It's time the world walked with Rosen.

References

Introduction

1 'Feminist protest as Playboy bunnies return', *Sky News*, 4 June 2011.

2 'Harnessing the Internet: the German porn king's revolutionary model', *Spiegel Online International*, 20 December 2012; 'How a (Canadian-founded) company you've never heard of took control of the porn industry', *National Post*, 24 October 2014.

3 '"King of Porn" arrested on charges of avoiding paying tax on the £60 million profits from his online sex empire', *Daily Mail*, 27 December 2012.

4 'Harnessing the Internet'.

5 'Online porn king Fabian Thylmann arrested for tax evasion in Belgium', *Gawker*, 10 December 2012.

6 'Hugh Hefner on his new documentary, and why all of his critics are wrong', *Vulture*, 2 August 2010.

7 '"Porn king" detained on suspicion of tax evasion', *Telegraph*, 17 December 2012.

8 'Porn's most powerful players', CNBC.com via Yahoo Personal Finance, 25 January 2013.

9 'BBC Three survey reveals one in four young people first view porn at age 12 or under', BBC Media Centre, 10 April 2014.

10 'Mega-brothels: has Germany become "bordello of Europe"?', BBC *Newsnight*, 21 February 2014.

11 '"Twice as many men" pay for sex', *BBC News*, 1 December 2005.

12 'Why DO women visit strip clubs?', *Daily Mail*, 17 October 2011; 'Strip clubs "may die out" if new lap-dancing laws come into place', *Metro*, 7 March 2010.

13 'From busts to boom: strip clubs say business is thriving',
   CNBC, 14 March 2013.

14 '*Cathouse: The Series*', IMDb (accessed via www.imdb.com,
   November 2015).

15 'Party Favors interview w/ Dennis Hof of HBO's Cathouse pts
   1 and 2', 20 October 2008 (accessed via YouTube, November
   2015).

16 'Here's what really happened to the cars from *Pimp My Ride*',
   Huffington Post, 25 February 2015.

17 K. Boyle (ed.), *Everyday Pornography* (Routledge, 2010), p. 1.

18 'Party Favors interview w/ Dennis Hof of HBO's Cathouse
   pt 1'.

19 'Nevada brothel owner to open Sci-Fi themed hooker house for
   men who want to bed women from out of this world', *Daily
   Mail*, 23 December 2011.

20 'Ending violence against women and girls', United Nations:
   Resources for Speakers on Global Issues (accessed via www.
   un.org, November 2015).

21 'Four in 10 teenage girls coerced into sex acts, survey finds',
   Guardian, 11 February 2015.

22 S. de Beauvoir, *The Second Sex* (1949; translation by H. M.
   Parshley; Pan, 1988), p. 29.

MYTH 1: *Demand for the sex trade is inevitable*

1 T. Hobbes, *Leviathan* (1651; The Folio Society, 2012), p. 40.

2 'France in passionate debate over prostitution bill', *Financial
   Times*, 29 November 2013.

3 Cited in T. Aquinas, *Summa Theologica*, Second Part of the
   Second Part, Question 10, Article 11.

4 T. Newburn, *Criminology* (Willan, 2007), p. 122.

5 C. Lombroso & G. Ferrero, *Criminal Woman, the Prostitute,
   and the Normal Woman* (translated by N. H. Rafter & M. Gib-
   son; Duke University Press, 2004), p. 221.

6 'Five years jail for bricklayer Lee Setford who "lost control" and

raped drunken woman at Beverley home', *Hull Daily Mail*, 2 July 2014.

7 '"You simply could not resist": Fury at judge's comments on convicted rapist', *Stylist*; 'UK judge thinks man who raped sleeping woman isn't a "classic rapist"', *Jezebel*, 5 July 2014; 'Judge to rapist: "You lost control . . . you simply could not resist"', *Cosmopolitan*, 5 July 2014.

8 'A personal choice', *The Economist*, 9 August 2014.

9 'On the city wall', in R. Kipling, *Soldiers Three* (F. A. Brockhaus, 1922), p. 240.

10 Cited in W. Hone, *Ancient Mysteries Described*, (1823; Redwood Press, 1970), p. 255.

11 See www.upworthy.com/about (accessed November 2015).

12 See www.facebook.com/Upworthy (accessed November 2015).

13 See www.facebook.com/Upworthy.

14 'It's time for legalized prostitution', *Slate*, 31 July 2014.

15 Lombroso & Ferrero, *Criminal Woman, the Prostitute, and the Normal Woman*, pp. 112, 113, 163, 126, 131.

16 T. Kemp, *Prostitution: An Investigation of its Causes, Especially with Regard to Hereditary Factors* (Levin & Munksgaard / William Heinemann, 1936), p. 47.

17 'Party Favors interview w/Dennis Hof of HBO's *Cathouse pt 1*', 20 October 2008 (accessed via YouTube, November 2015).

18 J. M. Keynes, *The General Theory of Employment, Interest and Money* (Macmillan & Co Ltd, 1960), p. 46.

19 Punternet review (accessed via www.punternet.com, November 2015).

20 C. E. Rissel et al, 'Sex in Australia: experiences of commercial sex in a representative sample of adults', *Australian and New Zealand Journal Of Public Health*, 27 (2) (2003): 191–197.

21 'What kind of men go to prostitutes?', *Live Science*, 25 March 2013.

22 'Almost one in 12 Irish men admit paying for sex', *Breaking News.ie*, 22 April 2015.

23 '"Twice as many men" pay for sex', *BBC News*, 1 December 2005.

24 M. Coy, M. Horvath & L. Kelly, '"It's just like going to the supermarket": Men buying sex in East London', report, Child and Woman Abuse Studies Unit, London Metropolitan University, 2007.

25 'Stop traffick! Tackling demand for sexual services of trafficked women and girls', report, Immigrant Council of Ireland, 2014.

26 'Men who buy sex: who they buy and what they know', report, Eaves, 2009.

27 'One in 10 British men have paid for sex, survey finds', *Huffington Post UK*, 18 November 2014.

28 'Tenth of British men "pay for sex"', *BBC News*, 18 November 2014.

29 Cited in 'Dirty young men', *Guardian*, 22 October 2005.

30 Coy et al, '"It's just like going to the supermarket"'.

31 D. M. Hughes, 'Prostitution Online', *Journal of Trauma Practice*, 2 (3–4) (2004): 115–131, pp. 123, 124.

32 'Paying the price: a consultation paper on prostitution', Home Office, 2004. See also: M. Hester & N. Westmarland, 'Tackling street prostitution: towards an holistic approach', report, Home Office, 2004.

33 'Paying the price'.

34 Hester & Westmarland, 'Tackling street prostitution'.

35 J. J. Potterat, 'Mortality in a long-term open cohort of prostitute women', *American Journal of Epidemiology*, 159 (8) (2004): 778–785.

36 'Stop traffick!'.

37 'Comparing sex buyers with men who don't buy sex: "You can have a good time with the servitude" vs. "You're supporting a system of degradation"', paper, Prostitution Research & Education, 2011.

38 Y. Katsulis, '"Living like a king": conspicuous consumption, virtual communities, and the social construction of paid sexual

encounters by U.S. sex tourists', *Men and Masculinities*, 13 (2) (2010): 210–230, p. 211.

39 Katsulis, '"Living like a king"', pp. 216, 220.

40 'Challenging men's demand for prostitution in Scotland: a research report based on interviews with 110 men who bought women in prostitution', report, Women's Support Project & Prostitution Research and Education, 2008.

41 'Deconstructing the demand for prostitution: preliminary insights from interviews with Chicago men who purchase sex', report, Chicago Alliance Against Sexual Exploitation, 2008.

42 'Men who buy sex: who they buy and what they know'.

43 R. Whisnant, 'From Jekyll to Hyde: the grooming of male pornography consumers', in K. Boyle (ed.), *Everyday Pornography* (Routledge, 2010), pp. 114–133.

44 A. Bandura, 'Selective moral disengagement in the exercise of moral agency', *Journal of Moral Education*, 31 (2) (2002): 101–119, p. 102.

45 Bandura, 'Selective moral disengagement . . .', p. 109.

46 'Comparing sex buyers with men who don't buy sex', p. 29.

47 Punternet review (accessed via www.punternet.com, November 2015).

48 'Reinforcing inequality: the need to challenge norms of development and the strip club industry as "progress"', S. Levêque, MSc in the Political Economy of Violence, Conflict and Development, 2008, p. 10.

49 'The real body of evidence', paper, Lap Dancing Association, 2008.

50 'Lap dance clubs may be limited', *BBC News*, 18 June 2008; 'The rise and fall of lap dancing', *BBC News Magazine*, 8 February 2012.

51 Accessed via www.viewlondon.co.uk, November 2015.

52 Accessed via www.viewlondon.co.uk, November 2015.

53 K. Frank, '"Just trying to relax": masculinity, masculinizing practices, and strip club regulars', *The Journal of Sex Research*,

40 (1) (2003): 61–75, pp. 65, 66, 70.

54 M. Flood, 'Men, sex, and homosociality: how bonds between men shape their sexual relations with women', *Men and Masculinities*, 10 (3) (2008): 339–359, p. 341.

55 'The Stag Company' (accessed via www.thestagcompany.com, November 2015).

56 K. Holsopple, 'Strip club testimony', report, Freedom and Justice Center for Prostitution Resources: A Program of the Volunteers of America of Minnesota, 1998.

57 B. Barton, 'Managing the toll of stripping: boundary setting among exotic dancers', *Journal of Contemporary Ethnography*, 36 (5) (2007) 571–96, pp. 580, 581.

58 Punternet review (accessed via www.punternet.com, November 2015).

59 M. Flood, 'The harms of pornography exposure among children and young people', *Child Abuse Review*, 18 (2009): 384–400.

60 'Nearly 80% of teenage males have seen sexual images online', University of East London press release, 30 September 2013.

61 'Is anti-sex feminism a step backwards for women's rights?', Feminist and Women's Studies Association Blog, 6 December 2013.

62 R. Whisnant, 'Confronting pornography: some conceptual basics', in C. Stark & R. Whisnant (eds), *Not for Sale: Feminists Resisting Prostitution and Pornography* (Spinifex Press, 2004), p. 20.

63 'Amateur hour: how the adult entertainment business turns fans into stars', *Complex*, 22 May 2014.

64 A. J. Bridges, 'Methodological considerations in mapping pornography content', in Boyle, *Everyday Pornography*, pp. 34–49, p. 37.

65 Cited in M. Tyler, '"Now, that's pornography!": violence and domination in *Adult Video News*', in Boyle, *Everyday Pornography*, pp. 50–62, p. 56.

66 A. J. Bridges et al, 'Aggression and sexual behavior in best-selling pornography videos: a content analysis update', *Violence Against Women*, 16 (10) (2010): 1065–1085.

67 Tyler, '"Now, that's pornography!"', pp. 50–62, p. 59.

68 'When watching porn, what is an instant boner killer?' (accessed via www.reddit.com, November 2015)

69 Bridges et al, 'Aggression and sexual behavior in best-selling pornography videos'.

70 Punternet review (accessed via www.punternet.com, November 2015).

MYTH 2: *Being paid for sex is regular service work*

1 'Unprotected: how legalizing prostitution has failed', *Spiegel Online International*, 30 May 2013; 'LobbyistInnen rüsten auf', *EMMA*, 6 December 2013.

2 'Unprotected: how legalizing prostitution has failed', 2013.

3 'Unprotected: how legalizing prostitution has failed', 2013.

4 'Report by the federal government on the Impact of the Act Regulating the Legal Situation of Prostitutes (Prostitution Act)', Federal Ministry for Family Affairs, Senior Citizens, Women and Youth, 2007.

5 'Wo wird das Gewissen abgestellt?', *EMMA*, 21 August 2013.

6 'The Act Regulating the Legal Situation of Prostitutes – implementation, impact, current developments', report, SoFFI K. Berlin, 2007.

7 H. Sporer, 'Speech for the seminar "Reality of Prostitution" of the European Women's Lobby on 1 Oct 2013 in Brussels'.

8 'Report by the federal government on the impact . . .'

9 'Report by the federal government on the impact . . .'

10 'A giant Teutonic brothel', *The Economist*, 14 November 2013; 'Germany rethinks its liberal ways on sex workers', *Guardian*, 30 November 2013.

11 '150 prostitutes and 50,000 punters, inside the world of Stuttgart's megabrothel', *Debrief*, 28 January 2015.

12 'Mega-brothels: has Germany become "bordello of Europe"?', BBC *Newsnight*, 21 February 2014.

13 'Welcome to Paradise: inside the world of legalised prostitu-

tion', *Telegraph*, 28 January 2015.

14 'Unprotected: how legalizing prostitution has failed', 2013.

15 'Unprotected: how legalizing prostitution has failed', 2013.

16 'Unprotected: how legalizing prostitution has failed', 2013.

17 'Welcome to Paradise'.

18 'Unprotected: how legalizing prostitution has failed', 2013.

19 'Raison d'être', *Jacobin* (accessed via www.jacobinmag.com, November 2015)

20 'The problem with (sex) work', *Jacobin*, 28 March 2012.

21 'The problem with (sex) work'.

22 'On that German legalisation of prostitution thing', blog, Adam Smith Institute, 3 December 2013.

23 'Why prostitution should be safe, legal and, well, not rare actually', blog, Adam Smith Institute, 16 July 2014.

24 'Prevention and treatment of HIV and other sexually transmitted infections for sex workers in low- and middle-income countries', report, World Health Organization, 2012.

25 'Understanding sex work in an open society', Open Society Foundations, accessed via www.opensocietyfoundations.org, January 2016.

26 'Ryanair long-haul flights have "blowjobs" included' (accessed via YouTube, November 2015). See also 'Membership of mile-high club goes on offer', *Independent.ie*, 19 June 2008.

27 'Report by the Federal Government on the Impact . . .'

28 'Report by the Federal Government on the Impact . . .', pp. 13, 14.

29 'Consent – what it means', This Is Abuse website (accessed via www.thisisabuse.direct.gov.uk, November 2015).

30 'Paying the price: a consultation paper on prostitution', Home Office, 2004. See also M. Hester & N. Westmarland, 'Tackling street prostitution: towards an holistic approach', report, Home Office, 2004.

31 M. Farley et al, 'Prostitution and trafficking in nine countries: an update on violence and posttraumatic stress disorder', *Journal of Trauma Practice*, 2 (3/4) (2003): 33–74.

32 M. Farley, J. Lynne & A. J. Cotton, 'Prostitution in Vancouver: violence and the colonization of first nations women', *Transcultural Psychiatry*, 42 (2) (2005): 242–271.

33 D. E. Roe-Sepowitz, 'Juvenile entry into prostitution: the role of emotional abuse', *Violence Against Women*, 18 (5) (2012): 562–579.

34 L. Plumridge & G. Abel, 'A "segmented" sex industry in New Zealand: sexual and personal safety of female sex workers', *Australian and New Zealand Journal of Public Health*, 25 (1) (2001): 78–83.

35 Farley et al, 'Prostitution in Vancouver'.

36 R. Matthews, 'Female prostitution and victimization: A realist analysis', *International Review of Victimology*, 21 (1) (2015): 85–100.

37 L. DeRiviere, 'A human capital methodology for estimating the lifelong personal costs of young women leaving the sex trade', *Feminist Economics*, 12 (3) (2006): 367–402, here p. 377.

38 'Information for survivors of sexual violence: dissociation', Rape Crisis Scotland, 2013, p. 3.

39 DeRiviere, 'A human capital methodology', p. 383.

40 K. Nixon et al, 'The everyday occurrence: violence in the lives of girls exploited through prostitution', *Violence Against Women*, 8 (9) (2002): 1016–1043, p. 1038.

41 Farley et al, 'Prostitution and trafficking in nine countries'.

42 'Sexual slavery in Mexico – a pimp tells his story', *Guardian*, 3 February 2014.

43 J. J. Potterat, 'Mortality in a long-term open cohort of prostitute women', *American Journal of Epidemiology*, 159 (8) (2004): 778–785, here p. 784, 783.

44 Hester & Westmarland, 'Tackling street prostitution'.

45 S. Church et al, 'Violence by clients towards female prostitutes in different work settings: questionnaire survey', *British Medical Journal*, 332 (7285) (2001): 524–525.

46 D. Whittaker & G. Hart, 'Managing risks: the social organi-

sation of indoor sex work', *Sociology of Health & Illness*, 18 (3) (1996): 399–414, here pp. 404, 405, 409, 412.

47 'A personal choice', *The Economist*, 9 August 2015.

48 'An Interview with Milton Friedman', *Chicago Life*, 1 June 2006.

49 D. Satz, *Why Some Things Should Not Be for Sale: The Moral Limits of Markets* (Oxford University Press, 2010), p. 16.

50 'Strategic plan: 2013–15', paper, Global Network of Sex Work Projects (accessed via www.nswp.org/, November 2015), p. 2.

51 'History', Global Network of Sex Work Projects (accessed via www.nswp.org, November 2015).

52 T. E. Nelson et al, 'Media framing of a civil liberties conflict and its effect on tolerance', *American Political Science Review*, 91 (3) (1997): 567–583, here p. 569.

53 'Feminist protest as Playboy bunnies return', Sky News, 4 June 2011.

54 See M. S. McGlone, G. Beck & A. Pfiester, 'Contamination and camouflage in euphemisms', *Communication Monographs*, 73 (2006): 261–282.

55 'The decriminalisation of third parties', briefing, Global Network of Sex Work Projects, 2013, p. 1.

MYTH 3: Porn is fantasy

1 'Date My Porn Star', Twitter profile (accessed November 2015).

2 'Some in porn business consider leaving Los Angeles after vote to require condoms for adult-film actors', *New York Daily News*, 18 January 2012; 'Porn industry may leave LA if city OKs condom use', *CBS News*, 18 January 2012.

3 'Online porn: evidence of its impact on young people', NSPCC, 6 April 2015.

4 '*Danland*: Slamdance review', *Hollywood Reporter*, 21 January 2012.

5 'New Tonight: *The Right Hand* premieres on the Movie Network/Movie Central', TV,eh?, 6 October 2011.

6 'XBIZ 360° drives adult industry consolidation', XBIZ.com, 24 January 2013.

7 '"Porn king" detained on suspicion of tax evasion', *Telegraph*, 17 December 2012.

8 'Porn is in rude health', *Guardian*, 7 June 2012.

9 'Pornography debate: just what's so terrible about a man looking at pictures of naked women? We all do it', *Daily Mail*, 2 April 2009.

10 'About us', The Site (accessed via www.thesite.org, November 2015).

11 'Porn vs reality', The Site (accessed via www.thesite.org, November 2015).

12 Criminal Justice and Immigration Act 2008 (accessed via www.legislation.gov.uk, November 2015).

13 Cited in M. Waltman, 'The politics of legal challenges to pornography: Canada, Sweden, and the United States', Stockholm University, 2014, p. 43.

14 K. Kapparis, 'The terminology of prostitution in the ancient Greek world', in A. Glazebrook & M. M. Henry, *Greek Prostitutes in the Ancient Mediterranian, 800 BCE–200 CE* (University of Wisconsin Press, 2011), pp. 222–255.

15 'Do it right', This is Abuse (accessed via www.thisisabuse.direct.gov.uk, November 2015); 'Consent – what it means', This is Abuse (accessed via www.thisisabuse.direct.gov.uk, November 2015).

16 'Advice about getting into the porn industry', We Consent (accessed via www.weconsent.org, November 2015).

17 '"King of porn" is unmasked by German taxman', *NZ Herald*, 22 December 2012, p. 5.

18 'Why I had to stop making hardcore porn', *AlterNet*, 7 February 2010.

19 'A rough trade', *Guardian*, 17 March 2001.

20 'Racism in the porn industry: the harsh reality exposed', AntiPornography.org (accessed via www.antipornography.org, November 2015).

21 'Is Doing Porn "Empowering' for Women?"' – Porn Lie #1

of 100 Exposed', AntiPornography.org (accessed via www.
antipornography.org, November 2015).

22 'Message to men who watch porn (and to those who are
trying to stop)', AntiPornography.org, (accessed via www.
antipornography.org, November 2015).

23 'Sex doesn't sell: the decline of British porn', *Guardian*, 5
October 2014.

24 'Advice about getting into the porn industry'.

25 J. Stanford, *Economics for Everyone: A Short Guide to the
Economics of Capitalism* (Pluto Press, 2008), p. 56.

26 'A resource pack for working with teens around porn', Planet
Porn, Bish Training, 2010.

27 'Planet Porn', Bish Training (accessed via www.bishtraining.com,
November 2015).

28 'Young people and porn – evidence', Planet Porn, Bish Training,
2014.

29 'Where do we see sexual images?', Planet Porn, Bish Training,
2014.

30 C. Itzin, 'Pornography and the construction of misogyny',
Journal of Sexual Aggression, 8 (3) (2002): 4–42, here p. 20.

31 Waltman, 'The politics of legal challenges to pornography',
pp. 139, 140.

32 C. Itzin, A. Taket & L. Kelly, 'The evidence of harm to adults
relating to exposure to extreme pornographic material: a rapid
evidence assessment (REA)', report, Ministry of Justice, 2007, p. iv.

33 M. Allen, D. D'Alessio & K. Brezgel, 'A meta-analysis
summarizing the effects of pornography II', *Human
Communication Research*, 22 (2) (1995): 258–283; Total number
of participants clarified in Itzin et al, 'The evidence of harm to
adults . . .'

34 M. Allen et al, 'Exposure to pornography and acceptance of
rape myths', *Journal of Communication*, 45 (1) (1995): 5–26.
The researchers stated that they did not detect a similar
positive association in non-experimental studies. However, in

2010, Hald et al reported, 'our reanalysis of the meta-analysis as originally reported by Allen, Emmers et al. showed that even in their originally reported meta-analysis heterogeneity indicative of moderators [of an association] was found despite their reporting of the contrary'. They further concluded, 'the results correct a glaring discrepancy in the research literature by showing that the relationship between men's pornography consumption and their attitudes supporting violence against women in nonexperimental studies are in fact fully consistent with those previously found in experimental studies focusing on the same association'. See G. M. Hald, N. M. Malamuth & C. Yuen, 'Pornography and attitudes supporting violence against women: revisiting the relationship in nonexperimental studies', *Aggressive Behaviour*, 36 (2010): 14–20, here p. 18.

35 Hald et al, 'Pornography and attitudes supporting violence against women'.

36 E. Oddone-Paolucci, M. Genius & C. Violato, 'A meta-analysis of the published research on the effects of pornography', in C. Violato, E. Oddone-Paolucci & M. Genius, *The Changing Family and Child Development* (Ashgate, 2000), pp. 51, 48.

37 Itzin et al, 'The evidence of harm to adults . . .', pp. 26, 20.

38 D. Zillmann & J. Bryant, 'Pornography, sexual callousness, and the trivialisation of rape', *Journal of Communication*, 32 (4) (1982): 10–21.

39 M. A. Milburn, R. Mather & S. D. Conrad, 'The effects of viewing R-rated movie scenes that objectify women on perceptions of date rape', *Sex Roles*, 43 (9/10) (2000): 645–664, here p. 645.

40 P. J. Wright & M. Funk, 'Pornography consumption and opposition to affirmative action for women: a prospective study', *Psychology of Women Quarterly*, 38 (2) (2014): 208–221.

41 N. M. Malamuth, T. Addison & M. Koss, 'Pornography and sexual aggression: are there reliable effects and can we understand them?', *Annual Review of Sex Research*, 11 (1) (2000): 26–91.

42 J. Hinson Shope, 'When words are not enough: the search for the effect of pornography on abused women', *Violence Against Women*, 10 (1) (2004): 56–72.

43 C. Sun et al, 'Pornography and the male sexual script: an analysis of consumption and sexual relations', *Archives of Sexual Behavior* (2014): 1–12, here p. 1.

44 Malamuth et al, 'Pornography and sexual aggression', p. 53.

45 Milburn et al, 'The effect of viewing R-rated movie scenes . . .'

46 Sun et al, 'Pornography and the Male Sexual Script'.

47 Wright & Funk, 'Pornography consumption and opposition to affirmative action for women', p. 216.

48 K. M. Swartout, 'The company they keep: how peer networks influence male sexual aggression', *Psychology of Violence*, 3 (2) (2013): 157–171.

49 N. M. Malamuth, 'Pornography's impact on male adolescents', *Adolescent Medicine: State of the Art Reviews*, 4 (3) (1993): 563–576, here p. 573.

50 Waltman, 'The politics of legal challenges to pornography', p. 103

51 'The feminist pornographer', *Salon*, 24 February 2013.

52 'Is Anti-Sex Feminism . . .?', 2013.

53 R. J. Berger, P. Searles & C. E. Cottle, 'Ideological contours of the contemporary pornography debate: divisions and alliances', *Frontiers: A Journal of Women Studies*, 11 (2/3) (1990): 30–38, here p. 33.

54 C. Sun et al, 'A comparison of male and female directors in popular pornography: what happens when women are at the helm', *Psychology of Women Quarterly*, 32 (2008): 312–325.

55 Sun et al, 'A comparison of . . .'

56 Sun et al, 'A comparison of . . .', p. 322.

57 'What is feminist porn?', Pucker Up (accessed via www.puckerup.com, November 2015).

58 'The Porn King', Forbes, 7 March 2005 (accessed via www.forbes.com, November 2015).

59 PuckerUp.com (accessed via www.puckerup.com, November 2015).

60 'So, what is feminist porn? Find out from a woman who makes it', *Cosmopolitan*, 6 November 2013.

61 'Judging criteria for FPAs', Feminist Porn Awards (accessed via www.feministpornawards.com, November 2015).

62 'The Oscars of porn', *Sydney Morning Herald*, 9 January 2006.

63 Accessed via www.cduniverse.com, November 2015.

64 'Award winners: 2015 winners', XBIZ Awards (accessed via www. xbizawards.xbiz.com, November 2015).

MYTH 4: *Objecting to the sex trade makes you a pearl-clutching, sexually conservative prude*

1 'Should lads mags be forced to hide their cover?', *5 News*, 29 July 2013.

2 'Laurie Penny: the most harmful effects of prostitution are caused by its criminality', *New Statesman*, 13 December 2012.

3 '"Hands off our clients!": an activism and advocacy guide for challenging the "Swedish Model" of criminalising the clients of sex workers in Europe', International Committee on the Rights of Sex Workers in Europe, p. 3:8.

4 '"Hands off our clients!"', p. 2:18.

5 'Internet porn "name change plan"', *BBC Newsbeat*, 26 June 2008.

6 'Is anti-sex feminism a step backwards for women's rights?', Feminist and Women's Studies Association blog, 6 December 2013.

7 'Is anti-sex feminism . . .?', 2013.

8 M. Farley, 'Prostitution and trafficking in nine countries: an update on violence and posttraumatic stress disorder', *Journal of Trauma Practice*, 2 (3/4) (2003): 33–74. This study of prostitution in nine countries found 89% of people involved in the trade wanted to leave it.

9 'Mission & Principles', Red Umbrella Fund (accessed via www. redumbrellafund.org, November 2015).

10 'Mission & Principles'.

11 Oxford Dictionaries (accessed via www.oxforddictionaries.com, November 2015).

12 SPACE International (accessed via www.spaceinternational.ie, November 2015)

13 'The soapbox: the '80s called and they want their sex wars back', *The Frisky*, 10 April 2014.

14 'Pornography debate: just what's so terrible about a man looking at pictures of naked women? We all do it', *Daily Mail*, 2 April 2009.

15 'A personal choice', *The Economist*, 9 August 2015.

16 'Dirty young men', *Guardian*, 22 October 2005.

17 C. A. MacKinnon, *Feminism Unmodified: Discourses on Life and Law* (Harvard University Press, 1987), p. 219.

18 '*The People vs. Larry Flynt* sparks protest', *Entertainment Weekly*, 27 January 2014.

MYTH 5: *Decriminalise the entire prostitution trade and you make women safe*

1 'Global gender gap report 2014', World Economic Forum, 2014.

2 'Legalise prostitution in 2010 – MP', *IOL News*, 30 January 2008.

3 'SA prostitution plans condemned', *BBC News*, 16 July 2008.

4 'SA mulls prostitution law ahead of 2010', *Mail & Guardian*, 22 June 2009.

5 'Convention on the Elimination of All Forms of Discrimination against Women', United Nations Treaty Collection (accessed via www.treaties.un.org, November 2015).

6 'To anyone using our daughter's legacy' (accessed via www.missingpeople.net, November 2015).

7 Cited in J. Outshoorn, 'Voluntary and forced prostitution: the "realistic approach" of The Netherlands', in J. Outshoorn (ed.), *The Politics of Prostitution: Women's Movements, Democratic States and the Globalisation of Sex Commerce* (Cambridge

University Press, 2004), p. 185.

8 L. Kelly, M. Coy & R. Davenport, 'Shifting sands: a comparison of prostitution regimes across nine countries', report, Child and Woman Abuse Studies Unit, London Metropolitan University, 2009, p. 23.

9 'Report by the Federal Government on the impact of the Act Regulating the Legal Situation of Prostitutes (Prostitution Act)', Federal Ministry for Family Affairs, Senior Citizens, Women and Youth, 2007, p. 8.

10 'Report by the Federal Government on the impact . . .', p. 9.

11 'Report of the Prostitution Law Review Committee on the operation of the Prostitution Reform Act 2003', Ministry of Justice, New Zealand Government, 2008, p. 29.

12 'Sex work and the law: understanding legal frameworks and the struggle for sex work law reforms', briefing, Global Network of Sex Work Projects, 2014, p. 6.

13 Prostitution Reform Act 2003 (accessed via www.legislation. govt.nz, November 2015).

14 'Prostitution in The Netherlands since the lifting of the brothel ban', report, A. L. Daalder, Research and Documentation Centre, 2007.

15 'Prostitution in the Netherlands . . .', p. 41.

16 'Report by the Federal Government on the impact . . .', p. 16.

17 'Unprotected: how legalizing prostitution has failed', *Spiegel Online International*, 30 May 2013.

18 'Unprotected: how legalizing prostitution has failed'.

19 'Report by the Federal Government on the impact . . .', p. 9.

20 'Prostitution in The Netherlands . . .', p. 13.

21 'Prostitution in The Netherlands . . .', p. 79.

22 'Prostitution in The Netherlands . . .' p. 55.

23 W. Huisman & E. R. Kleemans, 'The challenges of fighting sex trafficking in the legalized prostitution market of the Netherlands', *Crime, Law and Social Change*, 61 (2) (2014): 215–228, here p. 226.

STATE

24 'Nearly 50 red light windows refused permit renewal in Amsterdam', *NL Times*, 19 September 2014.
25 J. Raphael, J. Ashley Reichert & M. Powers, 'Pimp control and violence: domestic sex trafficking of chicago women and girls', *Women & Criminal Justice*, 20 (1–2) (2010): 89–104, here p. 97.
26 M. Verhoeven et al, 'Relationships between suspects and victims of sex trafficking: exploitation of prostitutes and domestic violence parallels in Dutch trafficking cases', *European Journal on Criminal Policy and Research*, 21 (1) (2015): 49–64, here p. 50, 56, 57, 58, 59.
27 'Report by the Federal Government on the impact . . .', p. 12.
28 'Report by the Federal Government on the impact . . .', p. 52.
29 H. Sporer, 'Speech for the seminar "Reality of Prostitution" of the European Women's Lobby on 1 Oct 2013 in Brussels'.
30 Sporer, 'Speech for the seminar . . .'
31 '18 Myths on Prostitution', briefing, European Women's Lobby, 2014.
32 'The SNEEP case', LJN: BD6972, Almelo District Court, 08/963001-07 print judgement, 11 July 2008.
33 '18 myths on prostitution'.
34 'Amsterdam tries upscale fix for red-light district crime', *New York Times*, 24 February 2008.
35 W. Huisman & E. R. Kleemans, 'The challenges of fighting sex trafficking in the legalized prostitution market of The Netherlands', *Crime, Law and Social Change*, 61 (2) (2014): 215–228, here p. 215, 227.
36 S-Y. Cho, A. Dreher & E. Neumayer, 'Does Legalized Prostitution Increase Human Trafficking?', *World Development*, 41 (1) (2013): 67–82.
37 N. Jakobsson & A. Kotsadam, 'The law and economics of international sex slavery: prostitution laws and trafficking for sexual exploitation', *European Journal of Law and Economics*, 35 (1) (2013): 87–107, here pp. 87, 102.

REFERENCES

38 'Ten reasons to decriminalize sex work', briefing, Open Society
    Foundations, 2012.
39 'Ten reasons . . .', pp. 1, 3.
40 'A guide to occupational health and safety in the New Zealand
    sex industry', Occupational Safety and Health Service,
    Department of Labour, 2004, pp. 53, 37, 40.
41 'Report of the Prostitution Law Review Committee . . .', p. 14.
42 'Report of the Prostitution Law Review Committee . . .', p. 46.
43 'Report of the Prostitution Law Review Committee . . .', p. 25.
44 'Report of the Prostitution Law Review Committee . . .', pp. 45,
    57, 122.
45 'Report of the Prostitution Law Review Committee . . .'p. 91.
46 'Report of the Prostitution Law Review Committee . . .' pp. 14, 94.
47 L. Kelly, M. Coy & R. Davenport, 'Shifting sands: a
    comparison of prostitution rgimes across nine countries',
    report, Child and Woman Abuse Studies Unit, London
    Metropolitan University, 2009, p. 52.
48 Report of the Prostitution Law Review Committee on the
    Operation of the Prostitution Reform Act 2003, Ministry of
    Justice, New Zealand government, 2008, p. 175.
49 '18 myths on prostitution'.
50 Prostitution Reform Act 2003 (accessed via www.legislation.
    govt.nz, November 2015), p. 26.
51 'Report by the Federal Government on the impact . . .', p. 9.
52 'Report by the Federal Government on the impact . . .', pp. 24,
    27.
53 'Report of the Prostitution Law Review Committee . . .', p. 151.
54 'Prostitution in The Netherlands . . .', p. 14.
55 'Report of the Prostitution Law Review Committee . . .', p. 156.
56 'A guide to occupational health and safety in the New Zealand
    sex industry', p.17.
57 'The Act Regulating the Legal Situation of Prostitutes –
    implementation, impact, current developments', report, SoFFI
    K. Berlin, 2007.

58 'Report by the Federal Government on the Impact . . .' p. 62.
59 'The Act Regulating the Legal Situation of Prostitutes – implementation, impact, current developments', p. 25.
60 'Report by the Federal Government on the impact . . .', p. 63.
61 'Report of the Prostitution Law Review Committee . . .', p. 109.
62 'Report of the Prostitution Law Review Committee . . .', pp. 17, 50, 123, 131.
63 'Report of the Prostitution Law Review Committee . . .', p. 154.
64 'Report of the Prostitution Law Review Committee . . .', p. 39.
65 Kelly et al, 'Shifting sands', p. 37.
66 M. Coy, M. Horvath, L. Kelly, '"It's just like going to the supermarket": men buying sex in East London', report, Child and Woman Abuse Studies Unit, London Metropolitan University, 2007, p. 25.
67 'Report of the Prostitution Law Review Committee . . .', p. 41, 29, 118.
68 Kelly et al, 'Shifting sands', p. 27.
69 'Report of the Prostitution Law Review Committee . . .', p. 167.
70 'Population clock', Statistics New Zealand (accessed via http://www.stats.govt.nz, November 2015).
71 'Report by the Federal Government on the impact . . .', p. 34, 79.
72 'Prostitution in The Netherlands . . .', p. 15.
73 'Report of the Prostitution Law Review Committee . . .', pp. 79, 80, 81; confirmation of the total number of local authorities at the time of the Prostitution Law Review Committee's research provided via email correspondence by the Ministry of Justice, June 2015.
74 'Prevention and treatment of HIV and other sexually transmitted infections for sex workers in low- and middle-income countries', report, World Health Organization, 2012, p. 8.
75 'Global movement votes to adopt policy to protect human rights of sex workers', *Amnesty International News*, 11 August 2015.

REFERENCES

76 'Alejandra Gil, Madama de Sullivan, recibe 15 años de cárcel',
   Excelsior, 13 March 2015. Translation by Translator UK.
77 'Dan 15 años de prisión a mujer que controlaba trata de
   personas en el DF', *Animal Politico*, 12 March 2015. Translation
   by Translator UK.
78 'Sex trafficking ring from Mexico to New York discovered',
   Huffington Post, 6 April 2012.
79 'Sentencian a 15 años de cárcel a la "Madame de Sullivan"', *El
   Financiero*, 12 March 2015. Translation by Translator UK.
80 'Prevention and treatment of HIV and other sexually
   transmitted infections for sex workers in low- and middle-
   income countries', p. 3.
81 'Terms of reference: UNAIDS Advisory Group on HIV and Sex
   Work' (accessed via www.nswp.org, November 2015).
82 'UNAIDS guidance note: HIV and sex work', report, UNAIDS,
   April 2007, pp. 2, 4.
83 'Global Working Group on HIV and Sex Work policy letter to
   Peter Piot September 2007' (accessed November 2015 via www.
   nswp.org).
84 'UNAIDS advisory group', Global Network of Sex Work
   Projects (accessed via www.nswp.org, November 2015).
85 '1st meeting of the UNAIDS Advisory Group on HIV and
   Sex Work', 4–6 November 2009, Palais des Nations, Geneva,
   Note for Record (accessed November 2015 via www.nswp.org)
86 'UNAIDS guidance note on HIV and sex work', report,
   UNAIDS, 2009–2012, Annex, pp. 6, 10.
87 'Draft policy on state obligations to respect, protect and fulfil
   the human rights of sex workers', Amnesty International,
   2015.
88 'Draft policy on state obligations . . .'.
89 'Sex workers' rights are human rights', Amnesty International
   news, 14 August 2015.
90 'Report of the Prostitution Law Review Committee . . .', p. 166.
91 M. Waltman, 'Sweden's prohibition of purchase of sex: the law's

reasons, impact, and potential', *Women's Studies International Forum*, 34 (2011): 449–474.

92 Waltman, 'Sweden's prohibition of purchase sex', p. 450.

93 'The real impact of the Swedish model on sex workers: advocacy toolkit', Global Network of Sex Work Projects, 2014, pp. 1, 1:1.

94 'Selected extracts of the Swedish government report SOU 2010:49: "The Ban against the Purchase of Sexual Services. An evaluation 1999–2008"', Swedish Institute, 2010.

95 Waltman, 'Sweden's prohibition of purchase sex'.

96 Waltman, 'Sweden's prohibition of purchase sex'.

97 'Evaluering av forbudet mot kjøp av seksuelle tjenester', report 2014/30, Vista Analyse, 2014.

98 Waltman, 'Sweden's prohibition of purchase sex'.

99 'Summary: Evaluation of the ban on purchase of sexual services', SOU 2010:49, 2010, p. 37.

100 'Evaluering av forbudet mot kjøp av seksuelle tjenester', p. 14.

101 'Prostitution, trafficking and modern slavery in Europe', Council of Europe Parliamentary Assembly, Resolution 1983 (2014): 12.1.1.

102 R. Surtees, 'Traffickers and trafficking in southern and eastern Europe: considering the other side of human trafficking', *European Journal of Criminology*, 5 (1) (2008): 39–68, pp. 47, 48.

103 Waltman, 'Sweden's prohibition of purchase sex'.

104 'Securitas-vd dömd för sexköp', Realtid.se, 30 June 2011.

105 'Top prosecutor nabbed in prostitution sting', *The Local*, 26 February 2013.

106 '"Hands off our clients!": an activism and advocacy guide for challenging the 'Swedish model' of criminalising the clients of sex workers in Europe', International Committee on the Rights of Sex Workers in Europe, p. 2:18.

107 '"Hands off our clients!", pp. 3:11, 3:15.

108 'Selected extracts of the Swedish government report . . .', p. 9.

109 'Evaluering av forbudet mot kjøp av seksuelle tjenester', p. 11.

110 'Human Trafficking and Exploitation (Further Provisions and Support for Victims) Bill: International Union of Sex Workers', Northern Ireland Assembly, Committee for Justice, official report (Hansard), 9 January 2014.

111 'Human trafficking and exploitation . . .', 2014.

112 'Human trafficking and exploitation . . .', 9 January 2014.

113 Population figures from 'Population counter', Statistics Netherlands (accessed via www.cbs.nl/en-GB, September 2015); 'Population statistics', Statistics Sweden, website (accessed via www.scb.se/en_, September 2015).

114 'Committee is briefed on trafficking bill', Democracy Live (accessed via www.bbc.co.uk/democracylive, November 2015), 16 January 2014.

115 'Ten reasons . . .', p. 1.

116 'Evaluation research report for Ipswich/ Suffolk Prostitution Strategy 2007–2012: EVISSTA 2', University of East Anglia, 2012, p. 2.

117 K. Wahlberg, Speech at the Third Swedish-Dutch Conference on Gender Equality: Trafficking in Human Beings and Prostitution, The Netherlands, 6 December, 2010.

118 'Chow brothers' high-rise brothel wins building approval', *NZ Herald*, 1 December 2012; 'Chows' super-brothel plan is off', *NZ Herald*, 30 March 2014.

119 'Prostitution in the Netherlands . . .', p. 79.

120 'Unprotected: how legalizing prostitution has failed'.

MYTH 6: Resistance is futile

1 'Just like death and taxes, pornography is here to stay', *Observer*, 8 February 2004.

2 'AWID calls for the voices of sex workers to be heard by the European Parliament', *AWID news*, 26 February 2014.

3 'The Red Umbrella Fund', Mama Cash (accessed via www. mamacash.org, November 2015).

4 'Apply for a grant', Red Umbrella Fund (accessed via www. redumbrellafund.org, November 2015).

5 'Global movement votes to adopt policy to protect human rights of sex workers', *Amnesty International News*, 11 August 2015.

6 AWID, Twitter, 11 August 2015.

7 P. G. Zimbardo & M. R. Leippe, *The Psychology of Attitude Change and Social Influence* (McGraw-Hill, 1991), p. 215.

8 '*Maxim*'s "Cure a feminist" spreads the sexism even farther than it dared hope', *Bitch Media*, 26 March 2012.

9 'Was 2014 the year the lads' mag finally died?', *Telegraph*, 29 December 2014.

10 'Internext expo 2012 Las Vegas, Fabian Thylmann Managing partner of Manwin part3' (accessed via YouTube, November 2015).

11 See www.wedontbuyit.eu (accessed November 2015).

12 'Touche pas à ma pute!', *Causeur*, 30 October 2013.

13 '343 French sign "Don't Touch My Whore" petition', *Telegraph*, 30 October 2013.

14 'Dominique Strauss-Kahn battles new charges in French prostitution case', *Daily Beast*, 26 March 2012.

15 '343 French sign . . .'

16 '"Hands off my whore" campaign outrages France', *France 24*, 17 November 2013.

17 'The absurd folly of some anti-prostitution campaigners', Adam Smith Institute, blog, 2 June 2015.

18 ' About us', Adam Smith Institute (accessed via www. adamsmith.org, November 2015); 'The absurd folly . . .'.

19 'The absurd folly . . .', 2015.

20 D. Satz, *Why Some Things Should Not Be for Sale: The Moral Limits of Markets* (Oxford University Press, 2010), p. 51.

21 D. Martin CBE, speech in the Houses of Parliament at the launch of the End Demand campaign, 22 October 2014.

22 See www.bi-gegen-bordell.de (accessed November 2015).

23 L. C. Schlup & D. W. Whisenhunt (eds), *It Seems to Me:*

Selected Letters of Eleanor Roosevelt (The University Press of Kentucky, 2001), p. 2.

24 See www.marchepourlabolition.wordpress.com (accessed November 2015).

Acknowledgements

I've been extremely fortunate to have Sarah Savitt as my editor. Her incisive feedback and unwavering support were pivotal to this project. Many thanks also to the whole team at Faber, in particular Hannah Griffiths, Kate Murray-Browne, Kate Ward and Sophie Portas. I'm grateful to Rebecca Carter, my agent at Janklow and Nesbit, for being so wonderfully supportive of *Pimp State*, right from our very first conversation in St Pancras station about the idea of writing it. Sincere thanks also to The Society of Authors' K. Blundell Trust Awards, whose backing was invaluable.

I got stupidly lucky the day Sophie Bennett came to work at UK Feminista. The conversations we've had and campaigns we've run have been integral to *Pimp State*. Sophie provided insights, feedback and support at every stage of the writing process, not to mention hours spent reading and re-reading different versions of chapters, and fact checking their content. It's been an utter privilege to campaign alongside someone who so embodies that which drives positive change: honesty, integrity, tenacity – and overwhelming kindness.

The whole team at UK Feminista have been fantastically supportive throughout, with particular thanks due to Hannah Pool for being such an awesome Chair.

Countless people provided support and assistance during

my research. In addition to those cited in the text who so generously shared their experiences, views and expertise, special thanks go to: Alison Tunwell and Jonathan Woolley for German translations; Andrea Matolcsi at Equality Now; Corine Schans for Dutch translations; Dan Vockins and colleagues at the New Economics Foundation; Denise Charlton at the Immigrant Council of Ireland; Halla Gunnarsdóttir and the whole team at McAllister Olivarius; Inge Kleine; J.C. at antipornography.org, who was so generous with her time and support with interviews; Karon Monaghan QC; Dr Maddy Coy at the Child and Woman Abuse Studies Unit, London Metropolitan University; Marie, who I was extremely fortunate to have as my guide and translator in Stuttgart; Pierrette Pape at the European Women's Lobby; Professor Rae Langton; Rosi Orozco at the Commission United Against Human Trafficking; and Yeliz Osman for Spanish translation and assistance with research.

And, of course, huge thanks to my family as ever.

Also by Kat Banyard

ﬀ

The Equality Illusion

In *The Equality Illusion*, 'the most influential young feminist in the country' (*Guardian*) and UK Feminista founder Kat Banyard argues passionately and articulately that feminism continues to be one of the most urgent and relevant social justice campaigns today.

Structuring the book around a normal day, Banyard sets out the major issues for twenty-first century feminism, from work and education to sex, relationships and having children. She draws on her own campaigning experience as well as academic research and dozens of her own interviews. The book also includes information on how to get involved in grassroots action.

'Kat Banyard is absolutely amazing.' Bridget Christie

'Banyard's focus on action is inspiring . . . Read it. Share it. Give it to your mum, your daughter, your son, your brother, your sister, your dad.' *Irish Times*

'Cogently argues that equality remains largely a myth. Banyard has a highly readable style . . . It's a salutary reminder that politics remains the chief means by which women can challenge and change modern culture . . . I am wholly convinced: the sooner we all take on the battle, the better.' *Independent*